# C. T. Studd

Other titles in *Heroes of the Cross*

# C. T. Studd

## Cricketer and Crusader

**Kathleen White**

Marshalls

Marshalls Paperbacks
Marshall Pickering
3 Beggarwood Lane, Basingstoke, Hants, RG23 7LP, UK

A subsidiary of the Zondervan Corporation

**British Library CIP data**

White, Kathleen
    C. T. Studd.——(Heroes of the cross)
    1. Studd, C. T.     2. Missionaries——Great
    Britain——Biography
    I. Title     II. Series
    266'.0092'4         BV3705.S78

ISBN 0–551–01245–5

Phototypeset in Linotron Plantin
by Input Typesetting Ltd, London
Printed in Great Britain by Richard Clay (The Chaucer Press)
Ltd, Bungay, Suffolk.

# Chapter One

The clearing, which only five years ago had been dense, uninhabited forest land, was now filled again, but this time with a vast crowd of Christians, all natives of the Congo who had been won to the Lord by the efforts of the figure who lay in the simple coffin at their feet. Many chiefs from neighbouring communities swelled the ranks of the two thousand gathered there, not seeking precedence because of their rank but standing shoulder to shoulder with their brothers in Christ. Those natives who had known "Bwana Mukubwa" – the "Big" Bwana – most intimately had been given the privilege of carrying his body to the graveside. A sprinkling of white missionary colleagues, conspicuous because of the colour of their skins and more Westernised clothing, lowered him down into the dark, African soil. They assembled there, "all one in Christ Jesus" (Galatians 3. 28) to pay their last respects to a giant amongst men – a giant in physical stature and also in his faith and love for his fellow human-beings.

The setting for this unique act of respect and devotion was starkly simple. A backdrop of towering, tropical trees indicated the limits of the clearing. Several sturdy buildings marked the nerve centre of the mission station. Close by stood a circular hut made of split bamboos tied together with native string. It was thatched by a grass roof, and had a floor of dried mud but served as Bwana's home, housing his simple possessions. Over the whole scene burst occasional gleams of sun through the tropical storm, highlighting the sad faces of the mourners and yet, at the same time, accentuating the expressions of triumph and victory which broke out as the Gospel was preached over the open grave of this seasoned warrior in Christ's army. Perhaps some were reminded of the passing of one of Bunyan's immortal pilgrims, Mr. Valiant-for-Truth. "So he passed over, and all the trumpets sounded for him on the other side."

The early setting of Bwana's life could not have provided a more vivid contrast to the circumstances of his departure. Born Charles Studd, the third of six brothers, he spent his early years in a background of cultured affluence. His father, Edward, having made his fortune as a large-scale indigo planter at Tirhoot in Northern India, had returned home to England to enjoy a life of ease and luxury. Both in his first home at Hallerton in Leicestershire and afterwards at Tedworth Hall in Wiltshire (now known as Tidworth), he spared no expense to create an atmosphere of generous opulence.

Queen Victoria had brought a long-needed period of peace and prosperity after the conflict of the French Wars. The new industrial era was in full swing with developments in technology boosting the export trade to almost every corner of the globe. Large areas of the map could be identified by their pink colouring as parts of the far-reaching British Empire. Although poverty, degradation and squalor still existed amongst the uneducated working classes, people of Mr. Studd's position in society enjoyed a cushioned, protected and lavish existence.

At Tedworth, large numbers of servants ensured the smooth running of a well-to-do gentleman's country home. Labour was cheap as domestic service was often the only work that many young people could hope to get. Although wages remained ridiculously low, school-leavers welcomed the opportunity to join the servants' hall in a country mansion because it supplied food and somewhere to live, offering much more comfort and security than they had known in the primitive cottages where they had been brought up.

Consequently, gentlemen's sons, like Charles, were waited on by a retinue of servants. With none of our modern labour-saving equipment, heavy chores kept the domestics busy from early morning until late at night. Large, lofty rooms contained many pieces of heavy, carved furniture and fussy, decorative small ornaments which were a nightmare to keep clean. Charles and his brothers no doubt took all this for granted while they were growing up, accepting it as part of their lives without questioning the deep class divisions that existed. It was an age of paradoxes – of blatant materialism and wealth, and yet faithful church attendance throughout the population in Britain. Some, no doubt, went to worship as sincere Christians with deep rooted personal convictions but for many the reason for being seen at church was because it was expected of them socially.

One might have imagined that the six Studd boys and their two sisters would have spent the whole of their lives in this atmosphere of wealth and privilege. This seemed likely until a series of events, which on the surface appeared to be coincidences, but on closer examination could be put down to the work of the Holy Spirit, revolutionised their father's life and gave him a completely new set of values and standards.

On his first return from India, Edward Studd determined to indulge in his passion for sport, which he had not had opportunity for in the East. As he loved fox-hunting, he set about a course of regular training and such was his addiction and dedication to the pastime that he became Master of Hounds. Not content with his own achievements, he made sure his young sons were also instructed and it became a regular sight to observe them in miniature jackets tailored in the conventional hunting pink, trotting on their ponies to join the Hunt.

Another of his passions was for cricket but not even he could have foreseen the consequences of this absorbing interest on his family. In one of his paddocks he had a cricket ground laid out which was in constant use throughout the season. Various fixtures were made with other country house teams in which his three older sons were encouraged to take part as soon as they proved competent.

Through his fondness for hunting, Edward Studd became a lover of horses and a sound judge of horseflesh. His wealth enabled him to buy a string of racehorses. He had a course specially constructed at Tedworth where he would try the horses after training them. So professional was his involvement that he finally achieved his great ambition which was to win the Grand National. In celebration, he bought his wife and daughters beautiful pieces of jewellery.

So his life appeared ordered and settled in the yearly round of sporting and social events which filled the engagement diary of wealthy country gentlemen. Hospitable by nature, he still kept in touch with friends from his indigo planting days in Tirhoot, and invited them for meals either in London or at Tedworth. One colleague was Mr. Vincent who surprised his host by refusing to place a bet on a horse which Edward promised him was certain to win an important race. "You are a fool!" exclaimed Edward. "He's a very safe chance. I can't understand why you're not prepared to risk some money on him. Never mind, I'll forgive you if you come and have dinner with me!"

He couldn't account for his friend's sudden reluctance

to place a bet, but he did not know of the amazing events which had taken place in Mr. Vincent's life. He had missed the ferry boat one day, returning from the Punchestoun Races in Ireland. Faced with a lonely unplanned evening in Dublin, on impulse he entered a theatre which he noticed while out on a stroll, expecting a lively entertainment. Much to his amazement the artistes billed outside proved to be none other than D. L. Moody and Ira Sankey, two out-and-out American evangelists. Both the music and the preaching fascinated Mr. Vincent so much that he prolonged his visit to enable him to hear the gospel message again and again. Finally, kneeling by his side, Moody helped him to accept Christ.

This was no flash in the pan, nor an emotional response which soon wore off under the pressures of ordinary life. On the contrary, Mr. Vincent became a changed man. Not only that, he behaved like the four lepers outside the city gates of Samaria who exclaimed after they had witnessed the miracle of the disappearing Syrian army, "We have good news and we shouldn't keep it to ourselves," (2 Kings 7. 9). He, too, desired to share the Christian gospel with his friends.

However, although he was eager to share his new faith, he acted with tact and discretion. Agreeing to dine with his friend Edward Studd, he offered to arrange the entertainment afterwards. They made their way to the Drury Lane Theatre where, instead of a show or a play, Moody and Sankey were to speak. The place so crowded that only a few special seats were left. Using all his influence on an usher, he managed to obtain two and from that moment Edward's eyes remained riveted on the speaker. At the end, Edward turned to his friend and used the same words as the Samaritan woman in John 4. 29 who had been speaking to Jesus, "He has just told me everything I have ever done."

In spite of his first impressions, Edward also came to

no hasty, emotional decision about accepting Christ. It took more than one visit before he was thoroughly convinced by their eloquent preaching and acknowledged Jesus as the Son of God and his own personal Saviour. Once he had taken that important step, however, there was no room for half measures. Determined to leave no obstacle in his life which would interfere with his new relationship with God, he approached Mr. Moody for further advice. "Which of my leisure activities should I drop, now I have become a Christian?" he asked.

Very wisely, Moody did not reel off a whole list of pastimes which would now be forbidden to him, but just gently pointed out that any sport which involved gambling would prove a great hindrance to a practising Christian. In response to further questioning he advised Edward, "If you start trying to convert your friends and loved ones, God will take away your appetite for anything harmful or unsuitable. Soul-winning will become the most important passion of your life."

People who knew Edward well might have scoffed at that stage, knowing his addiction to the turf. Yet, so sincere was his change of heart, that he immediately gave up all his racing connections. His new attitude, needless to say, was commented on by his friends and acquaintances. They couldn't understand a man of such decided tastes suddenly turning his back on his favourite pursuits. It seemed extraordinary to them. It wasn't as though he had lost his fortune. Far from it, in fact he was now diverting his wealth into other channels! His coachman tersely summed up the situation when questioned about his master. "There's still the same skin, sir, but there's a new man inside!"

This "new man" gave his elder sons a horse each to keep as a hunter and then sold the others. What money he gained from these transactions he invested in his

Christian activities. In his mansion at Tidworth, he created a meeting room in the large hall and booked first class speakers to travel down to preach to an invited congregation, culled from all walks of life. Rather like the King's servants in the parable of the great feast (Matthew 22 1 – 10), he went out "into the country roads and lanes" and invited people to come in.

With Edward Studd's unflagging enthusiasm, it might seem more than likely that he would get in touch with his three eldest boys who were at school at Eton immediately he had become a Christian to try to persuade them to follow in his footsteps. As it happened, there was a short lapse of time before he wrote to them at the half-term holiday to suggest that they should come up to London to meet him. Perhaps the delay occurred because he had so much to put right in his own life first which he considered a priority.

Even after receiving their father's letter, the boys still had no idea about his profession of faith, so they naturally imagined he must have arranged a treat for them as usual, perhaps a dinner or a show in town. From Eton, it was a short journey for them.

Their reaction to their father's invitation was predictable for young fellows of that age. Initially, they could hardly believe it when they discovered they were expected to go with him to a Moody gospel preaching and then they weren't particularly interested. So their first introduction to the great evangelist did not meet with instant results. However, this in no way deterred their father from pursuing his objective. He felt confident it was merely a matter of time.

# Chapter Two

Glimpses of Charles in his infancy and childhood are tantalisingly few and far between. For anyone trying to write about his life, the source material is scanty. Fortunately his mother and his wife kept all his letters and these provided the basis for a biography by Norman Grubb, Charles' son-in-law, which was first published in 1933, and entitled, *C. T. Studd, Cricketer and Pioneer.*

His achievements are easy to describe but he himself remains a shadowy figure, austere and almost fanatical in his zeal for the gospel, particularly towards the end of his life. There are few human touches to help appreciate him as a person, and there are many gaps in our early knowledge of him.

Charles, however, was quite outspoken on one subject. "We were always glad when Sunday had passed and Monday morning arrived again. I used to think religion was a thing for one day only, in spite of being brought up to go to church regularly. The Sabbath was by far the dullest day of the week for us."

Although Charles had not become a Christian himself at that stage, he recognised the change in his father. It was for real with him – not just a hypocritical ego-trip. Charles called Edward "a real live play-the-game Christian." But although he appreciated his father's complete sincerity, he didn't always approve of his methods. "Everyone in the house had a dog's life of it until they were converted," he stated. He confessed to pretending to be asleep when his father came into his bedroom at night to ask if he had been converted, and also to hiding from him during the day. No doubt it made Charles feel uncomfortable, perhaps even longing for the good old days before his father's zeal was so relentless.

Fortunately, outdoor games were arranged as usual during the holidays. At least, Edward didn't deprive his sons of their enjoyment of sport although he still kept to his plan of inviting speakers down for the weekend. One of them to whom the boys took an instant dislike was a Mr. Weatherby. They despised him because they judged him to be rather timid and unsportsmanlike. However, later in the day he earned their grudging respect. Knowing he had little experience in horse-riding, they arranged for him to go out on horseback with their father. At a given signal, the boys all cantered past him at great speed, trying to frighten him and his mount, but Mr. Weatherby managed to cling on and finish unharmed, rather to their surprise.

In the afternoon, the tables were turned. Mr. Weatherby quizzed each of the boys about their Christian beliefs. What he said exactly to Kynaston and George is unknown, but Charles wrote a graphic description of his conversation. At first Charles kept giving him fairly vague and evasive replies, but Mr. Weatherby managed to pin him down in the argument again and again. Finally, he asked "When someone gives you a present at Christmas what do you do?" "I take it and say thank-you," answered Charles innocently. So Mr. Weatherby appealed to him to go down on his knees and thank God for what the Bible calls "His unspeakable gift," (2 Cor. 9 15).

Although people might have thought it unwise for Mr. Weatherby to press the boys about their faith in Christ, his sincerity impressed all three of them, and they each committed their lives to Christ. Charles stated afterwards, "Right then . . . joy and peace came into my soul. I knew what it was to be born again." The boys didn't confide in each other but wrote separately to their father on their return to Eton. His letters back to them made them aware that they had all come to the momentous decision on the same day. So Edward had three sons with the same spiritual birthday – and all in the same cricket team – the famous Eton XI.

It seemed as though Edward felt driven on by a great urgency, yet nothing suggests he had any premonition of his approaching, untimely death. He lived only two years after his conversion, but the time was crammed to the full with evangelising activities. He was anxious to spread the good news to as many unbelievers as possible and these, of course, included the members of his family and his staff.

Eventually, even the circumstances of his death could be traced to his zeal for witnessing on behalf of the Lord. On his way to another of Moody's meetings, he stopped his coach and ran back to fetch one of the grooms he had forgotten to bring with him. In doing so he broke a blood-vessel in his leg which caused his final illness. At his funeral service a single comment from the clergyman's sermon proves very significant: "He did more in two years than most Christians do in twenty."

Apart from his great wealth, he left his sons a much more valuable asset. It was not immediately apparent, but later in their careers they displayed the same dedication and whole-heartedness as their father in whatever activity they were engaged. This enthusiasm, added to their outstanding sportsmanship which their father had encouraged, and the first-rate education which he had provided for them, made them into stable, well-rounded characters.

Had Charles come from a working-class family, the loss of his father would certainly have altered his circumstances completely. Without any system of pensions or state relief, poor mothers were compelled to send their children out to work once the bread-winner had died. However, the question did not arise for the Studd brothers. Although sincerely missing their father the boys' lives carried on very much as usual. They may have felt the best tribute to his memory was to put all their efforts into their studies and sporting activities, and he would have been proud of the fact that they all gained places as undergraduates at Cambridge University. Charles drily admitted on leaving school, "I have learnt a great deal more through cricket than through books!"

The boys' cricketing career was a spectacular success. The three brothers kept creating new records in the sport. Cricketers are always careful to record statistics, so we have fairly detailed accounts of the matches in which they played. They were together in the Eton XI for only one year, but Charles stayed on there for two more years on his own as captain of the team. A report on the Eton-Harrow match of 1879 contained the phrase, "Incomparably the best cricketer was the Eton Captain, C. T. Studd."

In addition, the Studd boys started a Bible Class at Eton while they were still together, drawing in quite a few boys. This raises an interesting point, "Can religion and sport mix?" Another famous Christian cricketer sought to answer this question in his book, *Parson's Pitch*, nearly eighty years later. David Sheppard, now Bishop of Liverpool, wrote, ". . . I believe that health, strength, quickness of eye, all come from God. Success comes from God – and so too can failure. . . . I can make a duck or hundred to the glory of God – by the way I accept success or failure."

This was very much Charles' philosophy of life. Another striking similarity exists between him and David Sheppard. Both test match players in their day they were both stirred by an American evangelist while at Cambridge University. Charles by D. M. Moody, and David by Dr. Barnhouse whom in his book he describes as "a blunt and aggressive preacher from the United States."

"Not many mighty, not many noble are called" we read in 1 Cor. 1. 26. showing that God quite often just chooses ordinary people to carry out His work on earth. Yet from time to time, He does pick someone in the public eye who makes a great impression, particularly on young people. David Sheppard, with the help of all the news media of his day, became a popular hero to many in the 1950s and 1960s, and won their respect for his dedication both to the game of cricket and the cause of Christianity.

Charles Studd, even without the benefit of radio and television, still found himself a household name throughout the land.

He was not even content to excel in one sport but made a name for himself in racquets and fives, representing Eton in the Public Schools Racquets Challenge Cup. His finely-tuned body, disciplined by his devotion to games, was to prove a tremendous asset to him in later years when tough, physical demands were made upon it. Even in the privacy of his own bedroom, instead of relaxing he would practise strokes in front of a long looking-glass.

Obtaining his Cricket Blue when he went up to Trinity College, Cambridge as a freshman, by the next year he found himself playing with his three brothers in the Varsity XI. A brilliant future in the sport was predicted

16

for him and enthusiastic reports of his playing in important matches appeared in cricketing journals. With his brothers he made outstanding scores. In one match they gained 249 out of a total score of 504. In 1882, his third year at Cambridge, he was acclaimed as, ". . . someone who must be given the premier position amongst the batsmen of 1882."

One match in particular stands out in the annals of cricketing history: that between Cambridge University and the visiting Australian team. From the start it appeared doomed to failure and some club officials even felt it was stupid for Charles to accept the fixture and risk almost certain defeat at the hands of the Australians but, nothing daunted, Charles went ahead with the arrangements. Excitement rose to great heights when the Australians' first total was passed. When play resumed on Tuesday, excursion trains were put on from many areas, full of excited supporters, longing to see the Australians routed. Their optimism was rewarded when, after a stand by Kynaston and George Studd of 106 runs, and a later contribution by Charles who actually scored the winning hit, Australia was beaten by six wickets.

From that time, Charles' fame as a cricketer grew nation-wide. He played several other matches against the Australians and that winter was invited to play with the Test Team in Australia. Rather as a joke, a few ladies presented some ashes in a silver urn to take back to England as the visiting team had avenged a previous failure. This was the origin of the historic Ashes, in response to a humorous epitaph in the Sporting Times which had declared, "In affectionate remembrance of English Cricket, which died at the Oval on 29th August, 1882, . . . the body will be cremated and the ashes taken to Australia." What started off as a joke became an international sporting institution.

In 1883, his last year at Cambridge, Charles captained

the University XI through the season. He established several further brilliant records and won for himself the reputation of an outstanding all-rounder. Success had not come easily to him. It only sprang from long hours of tedious practice which helped to shape not only his cricketing prowess but his future character. No-one could have foreseen at that stage what reserves of courage and self-discipline he would have to call upon later in his life. Sometimes Charles, on looking back, felt pangs of regret that he had allowed the sport to become too big an idol in his life, but he never minimised his enjoyment of the game.

The three brothers established a record at Cambridge because George was captain of the XI in '82, Charles in '83 and Kynaston in '84 in unbroken succession. If that wasn't enough, Charles won the Cambridge single Racquets Match and represented Cambridge against Oxford.

When Charles came down from the University in 1884 after obtaining his B.A. degree, he wondered what the future held for him. The sporting life of any cricketer, however remarkable, was bound to be relatively short. Fortunately, however, just at that period he was becoming aware about the claims of Christ on his subsequent career. His privileged life, wealth and worldly success would pull him in one direction while his commitment to Christ would pull the opposite way. Which influence would win that spiritual tug-of-war?

# Chapter Three

Had Edward Studd been alive he would have been proud of Charles' meteoric rise to fame in cricket. His son's spiritual progress would have afforded him less satisfaction. True, on leaving Eton in 1879, his housemaster's report noted, ". . . he has done no little good to all who come under his influence," but on the whole his main energies were devoted to the game at which he excelled.

Perhaps Charles was too hard on himself when he wrote later, "Instead of going and telling others of the love of Christ, I was selfish . . . and gradually my love began to grow cold and the love of the world came in. I spent six years in an unhappy backslidden state." That was his own admission but he failed to add that he had certainly not cut himself off completely from Christian activities at the University. Occasionally he would join in a sing-song of hymns round the piano or attend one of the Daily Prayer Meetings. He even took Christian Union literature round to freshmen and made no secret of the fact that he claimed to be a Christian.

All this, certainly, proved an asset to the Christian nucleus at Cambridge. Charles had become a popular figure both there and in the wider world outside the university because of his sporting reputation. In addition he was kind-hearted, wealthy and physically handsome, so was a valuable support to any group with which he was associated. No wonder he felt the pull of worldly ease and enjoyment straining against his Christian commitment. It was easier to drift into a state of compromise than make a tremendous effort to be a distinctive witness like his father.

At least Charles was honest about himself. Many years afterwards he wrote to Kynaston, "I never forget the influence your life had upon me and how I admired your courage and loyalty to the Lord Jesus Christ . . . you were ever faithful in speaking to our cricketing friends about their souls," – a difficult admission for one brother to make to another. Charles knew in his heart of hearts that he had never won a soul for Christ and that he had become satisfied with a very nominal Christian existence.

But once God has called someone to follow Him, He does not abandon him at the first falling away of enthusiasm. God is never taken by surprise and He holds in reserve other servants, other plans to bring about His purposes. Just about the time that Charles had been selected to play Test Cricket in Australia two elderly ladies devoted themselves to praying that he should be stirred again in his Christian faith. Knowing his father in the past, they could see the potential in Charles if he only caught the vision of dedicated service for the Lord. But how was it to be brought about? They did not know, but continued to pray in faith.

And so it was that in 1883 God answered sincere prayer for Charles in a remarkable way. George Studd became ill, and this was to bring Charles back to his senses.

George's life hung in the balance for several days. As Charles sat by his brother's bedside in the darkened room, with straw laid down on the street outside to muffle the noise of carriage wheels and horses' hooves, as was customary in Victorian times, he had plenty of opportunity to reflect. For a few days he was away from the field of action, away from his friends, consumed by anxiety for his brother. The result was that Charles examined his standards and values and appraised them for their true significance. "God showed me what the honour, what the pleasure, what the riches of this world were worth." George had already learnt this lesson.

So, the beginning of the New Year, 1884, brought a new phase in Charles' life. "God brought me back," was the simple expression he used. To his great joy, George was restored to full health and strength. Almost immediately afterwards, Charles attended a meeting conducted by Mr. Moody at St. Pancras where he claimed, "The Lord restored to me the joy of His salvation."

This time it was for real and Charles seized every opportunity to spread the good news to other friends and acquaintances. He also took good care that they accompanied him to hear Moody in London or to other evangelistic services in Cambridge. Soon he experienced great happiness in persuading a close friend to become a Christian. "I have tasted most of the pleasures this world can give," he admitted afterwards, "but . . . they were as nothing compared to the joy that the saving of that one soul gave me."

Like his father, Charles never did anything by half measures. He carried out his Christian service with the same energy and enthusiasm as he had displayed in his cricketing career. All those long hours of practising in front of the tall mirror in his bedroom had worked up great powers of concentration and singlemindedness. As soon as the new cricket season began, Charles felt his immediate mission field was the cricket pitch. "I have found something infinitely better than cricket. My heart was no longer in the game; I wanted to win souls for the Lord."

Three outstanding members of the M.C.C. Test team accompanied him to hear Moody and were converted as a result. So far, so good, but Charles was already looking to the future wondering where his life's work lay. He felt sure God had prepared a blue-print for him.

While he and his brother Kynaston had assisted Mr. Moody in his meetings, and the cricket season had been in full swing, Charles had little time for brooding. But once the physical activity had finished for the season, Charles tortured himself mentally trying to find out the answers to his questions. In the end he took himself off to the country for three months to relax and sort out his priorities.

Mr. Moody had already returned to America, so Charles' immediate involvement with mission was over for the time being. Thinking over his affairs rationally, Charles first decided that he would read for the Bar until God revealed to him what his life's work should be. Even that decision did not satisfy him for long. "God had given me far more than was sufficient to keep body and soul together . . . how could I spend the best hours of my life in working for myself and for the honour and the pleasures of this world while thousands and thousands of souls are perishing every day without having heard of the Lord Jesus Christ, going down to Christless and hopeless graves?"

At this stage, Charles got down to regular and consistent Bible study. The words of the Lord Jesus came through to him quite clearly, "No man can serve two masters," Luke 16. 13, and, "No man, having put his hand to the plough and turning back, is fit for the kingdom of God", Luke 9. 62. One day in the house of a friend he heard of a Christian woman who, in spite of passing through a great deal of sorrow and trouble, always possessed an overwhelming sense of peace which helped her to face up to her difficulties.

"Why isn't it like that with me?" Charles asked himself in perplexity. "I'm a Christian, too, but I would give a great deal to enjoy her peace of mind. What's holding me back?"

It was then he realised he hadn't fully committed himself to Christ, and kneeling down he repeated lines from Frances Ridley Havergal's famous hymn:

Take my life and let it be,
Consecrated, Lord, to Thee.

Now Charles completely trusted that he had at last achieved the contentment and security he had so long been seeking. He was willing to accept any suggestion the Lord might put forward for his future. When he thought about it, he imagined it would be spent in England. After all, there were thousands, even millions, of his own countrymen living in sin, ignorant of Christ's salvation.

At this stage, a friend from Cambridge days came to call on Charles at the Studd's family home in London. Former Captain of the First Trinity Boat Club, Stanley Smith had already volunteered his services to the China Inland Mission. God had been speaking to him also over a number of months and he felt the sentence from Isaiah 49. 6 applied particularly to him, "I will also give you for a light to the Gentiles, that you may be my salvation to the end of the earth."

"Why don't you come with me?" Stanley asked Charles. "I'm going this evening to C.I.M. Headquarters. John McCarthy's having a farewell service before he goes back as a missionary to China. I'm sure you'd enjoy it."

Not only did Charles find it interesting and enjoyable, John McCarthy's testimony that "thousands of souls are perishing every day and night without even a knowledge of the Lord Jesus" pointed Charles in the right direction. Slipping away quietly to pray for guidance, God spoke to him through a text from Matthew 10, "He that loves his father and mother more than me is not worthy of me". That sealed his decision, even if it meant breaking his mother's heart, by leaving England.

He couldn't keep the secret to himself for very long. On the way home it came bubbling out to Stanley Smith as he sat chatting on the top of a horse-bus. Stanley was so overjoyed that he rushed back to share the news with John McCarthy and then wrote a letter to Hudson Taylor, the founder of the Mission.

It was harder, much harder, for Charles. He first told his brother Kynaston who wondered if Charles was doing the right thing. After all, he had been on a sort of spiritual see-saw for several months. The effect on his mother was worse than he had feared. Mrs. Studd became distraught at the thought of Charles going to China as a missionary. A friend writing about this afterwards stated, "Kynaston says he has never in his life seen two such days of suffering and sorrow" (referring to his mother's grief). She kept begging Charles to put off the decision for another week. The two brothers got down on their knees to appeal for further evidence of God's guidance. This did not bring Charles peace of mind. Sleep eluded him all night but next morning he set off resolutely for Mildmay, heartened by a text which the Lord had planted in his mind: "I will give you the heathen for your inheritance and the uttermost parts of the earth for your possession" (Psalm 2. 8).

Even after he had offered his services to the C.I.M., and been accepted by its leader Hudson Taylor, Charles still had to resolve an inner conflict. He had no doubts at all about what he wanted to do but was it right to upset his mother so much, particularly as she was a widow? The battle raged so fiercely within him that he got off the horse-bus, half-intending to withdraw his offer to the Mission.

At King's Cross underground station he stood on the platform, still praying for guidance. By the light of a platform lamp he was able to read the page at which his Bible had opened in his hands. The message proved clear and decisive. "A man's foes shall be those of his own household", (Matthew 10. 36). From that time on, he entertained no second thoughts or hesitations about his calling.

It was unfortunate that his brother misunderstood him and his mother could only think of her natural sorrow in parting with him. In those days a candidate for the mission field disappeared for years from his family, particularly when serving in remote countries like China. There was no quick flight home for a regular furlough. A long sea voyage provided the only means of transport home after years of arduous service. No wonder Mrs. Studd dreaded Charles' departure. It seemed almost like a death sentence. Would she ever see her beloved son again?

For Charles, however, there was no further conflict. If it meant hurting his mother, he felt very sorry indeed yet the only alternative was to disobey or disregard God's call and this, to him, was unthinkable. So the die was cast. He was wholly committed to the China Inland Mission. All that this would involve he did not appreciate immediately but his destiny and destination were clear – to win the Chinese for Christ.

Hudson Taylor had been challenged to missionary service as a young man when working in a warehouse. Later he trained with a leading doctor in Hull to equip himself with useful knowledge for the future. When he finally arrived in Shanghai in 1854 the city was in the grip of war and his financial resources were hardly sufficient to keep him alive. Incredibly, on his first furlough home after six years of service, Hudson deposited £10, the only money he possessed, as the starting capital for his China Inland Mission. No wonder Charles was attracted to a man of this calibre. He was a man after his own heart whose ideals and goals and determination identified completely with his own.

# Chapter Four

An internationally famous cricketer casting aside his career prospects in favour of humble missionary service was headline news. But an even greater phenomenon followed which fired the public imagination. Charles had for company his friend Stanley Smith, the stroke oar of the Cambridge boat, but they were not alone for long. Within weeks they had been joined by five other volunteers, all Cambridge University graduates. They became known as the Cambridge Seven and composed a formidable and impressive team which has never been equalled since.

Apart from Charles and Stanley, there was Montagu Beauchamp, the son of a baronet; D. E. Hoste, a gunner subaltern and son of a major-general; W. W. Cassels, a Church of England curate; Cecil Polhill-Turner, a Dragoon guardsman, and his brother Arthur. Theirs was no impulsive gesture but a rationally thought-out action by well-trained minds. Their names became household words in a remarkably short time. Even Queen Victoria herself graciously accepted a booklet which contained their testimonies. The eyes of the whole nation were upon these seven young men.*

Naturally, keen Christians all over the country were

*Their story is told in *The Cambridge Seven* by John Pollock. Published by Marshalls, 1984.

anxious to exploit this situation for good. Leading professors at Edinburgh University invited Charles and Stanley to address students up there. Once they accepted, the back-up team responded magnificently. Only the best arrangements would be suitable for Christ's service. Invitations were carefully printed on high-class notepaper. It was clearly stated that only students could gain entry to the Free Assembly Hall. Previously sandwich board men had advertised the event and this resulted in a completely full house.

The outcome of the meeting possibly owed as much to Charles and Stanley's earnest prayers in their host's drawing-room for hours before they actually addressed the students. Stanley waxed eloquent in his speech but Charles impressed all by his undoubted sincerity. His previous reputation as an international cricketer attracted attention although he found it difficult to put a speech together. Students crowded round afterwards to shake hands and learn more of Christ and many rushed down to the station, spilling on to the platform to wave "God-speed". People were convinced that a mighty movement of the Holy Spirit had begun but no-one could have foretold how widespread it would become.

The clatter of running feet alongside the moving train echoed throughout Waverly Station. "Will ye no come back again?" was the lyric which loyal Scots had sung to their departing Prince Charlie in the previous century after the 1745 Rebellion. This was the same sentiment felt by the students at Stanley's and Charles' departure.

Another meeting was soon arranged which produced equally powerful results. Before they left for China the Seven on many occasions spoke briefly and sincerely about their personal faith and many of their hearers were reduced to tears and counselling went on hour after hour. Students felt the urge to take the gospel message to other universities throughout the United Kingdom.

It might have been expected that Charles and Stanley would at that stage give themselves a breathing-space to relax and make their preparations for their journey to China. But a call came for even more strenuous efforts, "Would you two be prepared to make an evangelistic tour throughout England and Wales, perhaps with Hudson Taylor?" A tall order indeed but they accepted the challenge. Reginald Ratcliffe, a close friend of Hudson Taylor's, saw the potential of such a tour and set about organizing it. Such resources needed to be tapped before the team of missionary candidates set out for China.

They hardly needed advance publicity, their fame had gone before them. The sort of enthusiastic and rapturous reception accorded to well-known pop stars nowadays greeted these young evangelists. It became like a royal progress from city to city. Charles described the meetings in letters to his mother from Rochdale, Leicester, Liverpool and other towns and cities. Not only were lives of converts being changed, Charles' whole outlook was gradually altered. "Finding out about the poor," he wrote to his mother, "has increased my horror at the luxurious way I have been living; so many suits and clothes of all sorts whilst thousands are starving and perishing of cold, so all must be sold when I come home if they have not been before." Perhaps Charles was reminded of the Lord Jesus who told his disciples as he sent them out, "Do not take two coats" (Luke 9. 3.).

Apart from new converts being made, people who had been Christians for many years found themselves revitalised and wholeheartedly committed as a result of hearing Charles preach. Charles impressed everyone with his dedication, rising early in the morning for prayer and Bible study.

The time for their departure was rapidly approaching so arrangements were made for three great farewell meetings at Cambridge, Oxford and London – a truly epic series. The first was described in *The Record* as, "the most remarkable missionary meeting held within living memory at Cambridge." Professor Babington chaired the gathering. The Seven had asked for him, because, they said, "he is so large-hearted, he loves all who love the Lord Jesus Christ." Naturally it was well-supported. Most of the people in the congregation became not only intellectually but also emotionally stirred. These fine young men, who had all been at Cambridge, had given up the chance of brilliant careers for uncertain futures in a virtually unknown land and with practically no financial reward. It might have seemed like madness, but it evoked admiration from all sections of the community. Curiosity, too, had motivated some of the audience. What had inspired these missionary candidates to cut themselves adrift from their wealth and social standing?

Three people connected with the China Inland Mission spoke first, and then the Seven, one after another. Charles' last words were, ". . . God does not deal with you until you are wholly given up to Him, and then He will tell you what He would have you do."

The next night at Oxford, in the Corn Exchange, the hall was packed again.

A cold, wet winter's evening might well have dampened the ardour of many people intending to be present at the Exeter Hall meetings in London. Yet from all over the city three thousand people poured into the building while hundreds were turned away. A broad cross-section was represented there from simple labourers to the Seven's own relatives. Charles must have rejoiced to take his own mother to the occasion. Although desperately opposed at first, she relented eventually when she realised the depth of his commitment and became one of his staunchest supporters.

A large map of China hanging on the wall provided

the setting in front of which sat forty Cambridge under-graduates. All were intent on becoming missionaries. The Seven filed in to great applause and the proceedings began. After an introductory speech, the Seven spoke briefly and simply, one by one. Charles, the last to give an address, told the story of "how the Lord has sought and found me and led me back to Himself". The meeting ended with the audience singing the hymn which had deeply challenged Charles.

Take my life and let it be
Consecrated, Lord, to Thee.

As the organ thundered, every member of the congregation rose to his feet to participate in Francis Ridley Havergal's hymn of dedication. It was a truly fitting climax not just to one meeting but to a whole missionary crusade up and down the country.

The hour was already late as the hall emptied but each member of the Seven was expected to arrive at Victoria Station, the next morning, 5th February, 1885, at nine-thirty to set off on a long journey to China.

Final farewells to family and friends filled their remaining hours in England, together with packing last minute essentials. Did any of them take a last look at sports trophies or similar mementos? Was Charles busy oiling his favourite cricket bat before he finally placed it in storage, not knowing when or if he would ever use it again? Sports blazers, cricket caps and army uniforms had already been folded away in trunks. Whatever happened, one fact is certain that no regrets were expressed. None of the Seven gave voice to last minute doubts or indecision in a sudden panic. Theirs was no impulsive, immature gesture, but a considered course of action in direct response to a personal call from God.

Next morning, the guard's whistle broke into their

parting conversations and the Seven waved goodbye to well-wishers on the platform. The boat train steamed out at 10 o'clock, taking them on the first lap of the journey which would embrace Dover, Calais, Brindisi, Suez, Colombo and China.

"Will it last?" was the question in people's hearts who heard about the magnificent sacrifice the Seven were making. "It's all excitement and adventure at the beginning but will the glow remain? Will the enthusiasm peter out when the difficulties start piling up?" But fortunately, the future and all its hardship and suffering was hidden from the Seven as their boat steamed slowly along the shipping routes half-way across the world. "Take no thought for tomorrow", their Lord had advised in His Sermon on the Mount (Matthew 6. 34). They were learning to trust daily on the word of the Lord and His promises. Doubtless they would, to a man, have indentified with the prayer of Ignatius Loyala, who became a true believer over three hundred years earlier as he lay in a Spanish castle recovering from wounds received in battle.

Teach us good Lord,
To serve Thee here as Thou deservest,
To give and not to count the cost,
To fight and not to heed the wounds,
To toil and not to seek for rest,
To labour and not to ask for any reward,
Save that of knowing that we do Your Holy will.

It was a warrior's prayer but was not each member of the Cambridge Seven a soldier in Christ's army? And each one would need also every piece of vital equipment mentioned in Ephesians 6: the belt of truth, the breast-plate of righteousness, the shield of faith, the helmet of salvation and the sword of the Spirit to enable them to spread the good news of Jesus.

After years of patient struggling through which they each remained faithful, their personal achievements were considerable. William Cassels was consecrated Bishop of Western China in 1895 where he remained until his death in 1925. Stanley Smith and Charles met their death in 1931. Stanley worked in China first with the C.I.M. and then in a different capacity but still involved in Christian projects in China for the rest of his life. Charles' stay in China was the briefest of the Seven, owing to being invalided home after nine years because of ill-health. His subsequent missionary activities filled the rest of his busy life, however, in other spheres. Arthur Polhill-Turner only retired in 1928 and his brother Cecil earlier in 1900 because of heart trouble but he made many subsequent visits. Montagu Beauchamp worked there until 1911 when he became a Chaplain to the Forces in the First World War, revisiting China on three occasions after the Armistice. D. E. Hoste, the oldest surviving member, did not leave China until 1945, after suffering internment by the Japanese. His death followed the next year. He was worn out by missionary activities and the treatment he had received during the war.

# Chapter Five

It must have been a relief to have made the final break with England, family and home. However painful the wrench, once the partings were over they had the future to look forward to and the pleasure and support of each other's company. They could well have been excused if they had taken the opportunity afforded by the voyage for rest and relaxation, particularly in view of their previous hectic schedule of meetings and their forthcoming missionary service.

In those days, the trip would take several weeks which would give the missionary candidates a considerable time to get to know one another better. But none of them were strangers to one another and some had spent a considerable time together at Cambridge but the frantic rush of the last few weeks had proved extremely demanding and left few opportunities for any social functions. Also it afforded them breathing-space between the old life and the new, allowing them to become acclimatised to their new calling and situation.

A modern missionary volunteer in the latter half of the twentieth century would be whisked away from one country and arrive in another in a matter of hours rather than weeks and perhaps would previously have received a fair amount of instruction about the culture and language he or she was likely to encounter. Not so the Seven. For centuries, China held only limited openings for visiting Westerners. Its complex language with thousands of intricate characters was enough to daunt any language student. The little knowledge they had gleaned had come from Hudson Taylor himself, the founder of the mission, and a few of the people who had served under him there.

But the Seven were young, energetic, intelligent and resourceful young men, anxious to begin their new life. Full of joy and the power of the Holy Spirit, they couldn't wait until they had set foot on Chinese soil to evangelise. Why? Plenty of opportunities already existed all around them. Charles, with his companions, threw himself whole-heartedly into the task of communicating the gospel then and there on the boat. His letters home to his mother babble with infectious enthusiasm.

All the seven second-class passengers on board became Christians during the voyage – the Cambridge Seven ministering to seven ordinary men and women! Perhaps not a remarkable feat in itself as all were closeted together in a comparatively small area over several weeks so the passengers were easily accessible for conversations and discussions, but one of their number was "a Captain of an Indian steamer. . . . noted for lying, drunkenness, swearing and blasphemy". He was disliked by the crew and had made a point of poking fun at the Seven as soon as they embarked.

Hoste button-holed the man first but Charles soon followed. "I told him of the happiness the Lord had given me . . . he poured out his heart to me." Charles challenged him to come to a decision at that very moment but, realising he needed time to think, left him to consider what he had heard. After writing home to ask forgiveness from all his family with whom he had quarrelled, "he went down on his knees in his cabin and told the Lord Jesus . . . he was a sinner, and asked Him to receive and save him. The Lord heard and answered him, and he is rejoicing in fulness of heart."

Mrs. Studd must have rejoiced too when this letter reached her and she must have felt glad that she had withdrawn her opposition to Charles' calling. It was a healthy sign also that a movement which started in the rather rarefied atmosphere of an English University had become tough enough to develop in the rough-and-tumble of life on board ship. It was a robust faith available for men, women and children all over the world. Charles at that stage could never have guessed how far his personal faith would cause him to travel. For the moment, his primary objective was China and this occupied all his thoughts.

A significant fact of the Seven's relationship one with another was that Hoste prayed with the man the next morning, showing how they worked as a team. No-one wanted to take the credit for one person's conversion. It was a combined effort which changed the atmosphere on board ship. Several stewards were so affected that they also became Christians.

By the time the Seven had arrived in China, they had undergone a transformation in their appearance. Heads which once wore mortar boards, cricket caps and military helmets now sported skull-caps and pigtails. Graduates' gowns, cricket flannels and blazers and dress uniforms had been exchanged for padded cotton gowns, the typical Chinese dress. Hudson Taylor had adopted Chinese dress early on in his missionary service and now insisted on all C.I.M. workers doing the same. It made sense. Chinese nationals, particularly from remote areas, had made little contact with Westerners so their formal dress would have created one more barrier between them and the missionaries. "When you're in Rome, do as the Romans", was Hudson's formula for success.

Charles could see the funny side of this. In another

letter he wrote, "I have been laughing all day at our grotesque appearance . . . Monty, Stanley and I make huge Chinamen; it makes us very conspicuous, as Chinamen are short." Three of them had to sacrifice their precious moustaches. It was just as well they had retained their sense of humour. They would need this desperately later on when they no longer could enjoy each others' company, and faced suffering alone.

It took four more months for the Seven to reach their destinations in different parts of China. Such a vast country with such a large population could have absorbed dozens of teams of missionaries but the smallness of their numbers did not appear to depress them, but spurred them on to even more magnificent efforts. Communications were poor and journeys slow and uncomfortable. Even when Charles rested for a few weeks to restore his energy and learn a little of the language, the accommodation proved poor and dirty. Did Charles ever think back to his father's luxurious house at Tidworth whilst he lay on the floor on flea-ridden mattresses? Was he reminded of his father's magnificent hunters when he ploughed through seas of mud with a weary ill-fed mule?

At least, he never divulged any momentary regrets in writing home. On the contrary his letters vibrate with joy in spite of the contrast with his former life of ease and comfort. It is fairly safe to say that such was his peace of mind and joy in the Lord that he wouldn't have changed places with anyone in the world, however privileged. He never considered he'd missed out on anything, but rather gained an immeasurable benefit from throwing up his career, wealth and prospects to become a missionary candidate.

He wrote, "The whole town has been talking of the meetings here, in fact, the Lord turned it upside down." Then later, "It is so trying to be unable to speak one word, but what joy it will be when I can . . . and the first convert comes."

After travelling as far as Hanchung with the two Polhill-Turner brothers, a journey of eighteen hundred miles, Charles and his friends were moored on houseboats alongside each other for three months of language study. He made light of difficulties, laughing at the problem of finding a shoemaker who would be willing to tackle making a pair of shoes to fit his outsize feet. The wintry padded clothing was discarded in the fine hot weather for a pair of white calico pyjamas topped by a sort of nightgown.

Rats plagued them and nibbled at their few possessions. Charles went into detail about this in a letter to his younger brothers Reggie and Bertie at Eton. (It was hardly a subject to mention to his mother!) But, having described the nuisance that they were, he continued "by all means play and enjoy games and cricket . . . only take care that games do not become an idol to you, as they did to me". Having himself experienced life at a large public school, he knew only too well the temptations and pitfalls which he wanted his brothers to avoid.

The next stage of his journey north to Pingyang-fu took several weeks overland and it proved tough going. There Charles planned to meet up with Hudson Taylor but it required all his stamina and endurance to complete the trip. Sleeping on bare boards and rising at 2.30 a.m. to be off by 4.00 a.m., his party would try to cover a distance of eight miles on foot before breakfast. Naturally, all this travelling played havoc with his rather soft feet which were used to Western comforts. The shoes specially made for him were discarded, as also coolie sandals of straw and string which meant he had to finish the journey on bare feet, raw and blistered. Unfortunately, the two colporteurs who were his companions wanted to step up the pace and cover forty-eight miles in one day, followed by thirty-eight the next. "Each step was like a knife going into them," commented Charles, "but I never felt the Lord's presence nearer the whole time." The agony must have been excruciating but Charles' reaction was expressed in the following words, "One simply felt bursting with praise and wonder at how the Lord had enabled one to get there at all." Charles' standards were the highest and extremely demanding, and some were to find him difficult to work with, but he always met them himself first.

One foot became swollen and infected and began to seriously trouble him. Finally Charles asked one of his companions to anoint him with oil which he did after a session of prayer. Charles again had cause to praise the Lord as the foot improved from that time onwards.

A clear picture emerges of his first few months in China from the descriptions in his letters. Undoubtedly, his main priority was to enjoy an early morning time of prayer with the Lord. This habit persisted throughout his life. Norman Grubb, his son-in-law, discovered this, to his cost, years later when he first met Charles in the Congo. Norman asked for special prayer meetings for revival. Charles agreed and suggested 4.00 am as work and activities began at 6.00 am. "When shall we have our quiet times then?" asked Norman. "Why not earlier?" came the calm reply! When Norman rose at 4.00 am he heard the aged Charles already playing his banjo to Africans whom he had gathered together for a prayer meeting.

But all that lay far ahead. Charles at first was laying important foundations for the rest of his long missionary service. He appeared to thrive on austerity. "This is far the best life, so healthy and good, lots to eat and drink and good hard healthy beds, fine fresh air; and what else does a man want?"

Repeatedly he bemoaned the fact that his earlier years had been characterised by self-indulgence and pleasure-seeking. Perhaps it was difficult for him to see that the Lord had used even those years of addiction to sport to teach him discipline and self-denial. His body originally had been toughened and trained to meet the demands of cricket and riding but those same muscles were now serving him well in his long treks across mountainous terrain.

Far from shrinking from the responsibility of being left on his own at Chin-Wu for several months to keep the station open, he relished the chance of mixing solely with the Chinese. The time passed quickly in language study, reading and tract distribution, and Charles was at last relatively free from most of the trappings of his former Western existence. Even his wristwatch had to be sent away to the coast for repair so he arranged his daily time-table by the sun. Friday, the Chinese cook, fed him more than adequately for 4p a day.

Certain pleasant interludes made land-marks in his first few months in China and broke the long spells of solitude and language study. A conference was arranged where Charles met up with "Old Cassells" again. What stories they must have exchanged about their separate experiences! Then suddenly a more serious matter absorbed them. Charles' host, Mr. Adamson of the Bible Society, developed small-pox and the two friends nursed him through the illness. "The Lord is able to make one equal to all occasions . . . so we were able to do what would ordinarily be the most revolting things."

Then the political situation deteriorated. Riots flared up in Szchuan and hatred against foreigners forced them to flee for safety. Characteristically, Charles, with a colleague, volunteered to go into Szchuan, but the journey proved hazardous. Sleeping rough on floorboards in filthy hovels they eventually reached Chungking, to the Consul's amazement as guards had been posted at the city gates to exclude "foreign devils". At first the Consul was reluctant to keep them there, being fearful for their safety, but later he invited Charles to remain with him. This Charles did gladly, accepting it as "in the will of the Lord" although not understanding His purpose at the time.

# Chapter Six

Prior to his departure for China, Charles had arranged an interview with Hudson Taylor to discuss his financial affairs. As his father had died an extremely wealthy man, he knew he would inherit a considerable fortune at the age of twenty-five. Hudson Taylor wisely pointed out that two years still had to elapse before Charles would be old enough to claim his fortune. "Think it over and make your decision later," was his advice.

Charles had already made up his mind. In his opinion there was no other option for a Christian, for what had Jesus told His disciples? "Lay not up for yourselves treasures on earth." It would have been easy for Hudson Taylor as leader of the China Inland Mission to encourage Charles to donate vast sums to this Society, but he knew that God would grant Charles wisdom to dispose of his assets to the most deserving causes. So for the time being the matter was put in abeyance. It could safely be left.

Charles' twenty-fifth birthday found him in Chungking. Later in the month letters arrived from his banker and solicitor, informing him of the true extent of his fortune. Far from causing him to change his mind, Charles resolutely set about signing his inheritance away. An official signature was required on the document. "Isn't that wonderful!" gloated Charles. "Now I know why God wanted me to remain in Chungking. It's the only place I would have found an English government official to do this for me."

In his turn, the Consul too tried to persuade Charles against this course of action. To the human mind, it seemed a little short of insanity. Within two weeks, however, he agreed to sign.

The total amount was still uncertain, so Charles proposed for a start to dispose of £25,000. "God has promised to give an hundredfold for everything we give to Him – what a fantastic investment!" exulted Charles. In this frame of mind he wrote four cheques for £5,000 each and five for £1,000, all on the same day in January, 1887. Even today this would be an extremely generous gesture, but a hundred years ago it represented a considerable fortune. The four large cheques were sent each to Mr. Moody, the American evangelist and were eventually used to establish the Moody Bible Institute; to George Müller in Bristol to help with his orphan homes; to George Holland in Whitechapel working amongst the poor in London and to the Salvation Army in India. Five cheques for £1,000 each went to Christian workers in Dublin, in London and to Dr. Barnardo's Home. Charles certainly possessed a large heart and an all-embracing sympathy for the needy and destitute. Although stationed in far-off China, he kept in touch and supported the Lord's work in his homeland.

Other smaller sums were given mainly to the C I M but after all the transactions, £3,400 still remained. Later, in one dramatic gesture, Charles would empty his bank account totally, but that time had not yet come.

Meanwhile, Charles journeyed down to the coast to Shanghai, having finished his immediate work in the Western Provinces. It was his intention to travel back to North China but he wanted first to contact his brother George who was due in Shanghai a fortnight after Charles' arrival. For once Charles found himself unable to communicate with Chinese citizens because of their peculiar dialect in that area, so he concentrated his preaching efforts on the sailors of the British Navy who happened to be in the port at that period.

A fairly casual remark hardly alerted people of an impending change in his circumstances. "In . . . the Sailor's Home, where we had nightly meetings . . . I found one or two ladies . . . then there was a Mr. Stevenson, the Deputy Director . . . and there was a young lady." Indeed, Charles' first impression of her was that she had made a mistake in coming out to that mission field because she was suffering from heart trouble.

This particular young lady was called Priscilla Livingstone Stewart. Had her parents been prophetic in calling her after the great African explorer and missionary pioneer? Her lively appearance and personality did not tally with the accepted description of a Victorian single lady missionary. Irish by birth, she possessed bright blue eyes, a beautiful complexion and golden hair. "Religion's not for me," she had declared at one time. Independent and high-spirited, she had enjoyed a hectic social round, unwilling to commit herself to any narrow, austere way of life. She even went so far as to say, "I will never serve God, I will never love Jesus nor call Him Lord and Master". Yet, like the apostle Paul before her, she had to eat her own words later on.

Three times she experienced a nightmare with a vision of Jesus saying to her, "Depart from me, for I never knew you," but even this failed to change her attitude until she discussed it with a newly-converted friend. From blatant opposition she changed to humble, believing trust in her Saviour and consecrated her life to His service. At that stage, perhaps fortunately, she hadn't the faintest idea what such a step would entail. But a faint foreshadowing of future events made her aware of what lay in store for her because, as she opened her Bible for guidance, in letters of light there appeared these words on the page, "China, India, Africa". Priscilla could only surmise that this message might refer to her future one day.

Coming from a mainly male household, public school and then male-dominated University background, Charles had had little experience of young ladies. Naturally, he would have been taught to behave courteously and thoughtfully to members of the opposite sex whom he met socially at Tidworth or in friends' houses, but Victorian insistence on chaperones left little opportunity for young men and women to enjoy each other's company for long.

The niceties of polite society were relaxed somewhat in missionary lifestyles abroad. Charles, for example, had received a letter from his friend Booth Tucker, working with the Salvation Army in India. In it he described how women led meetings, provided meals and organised whole bands of new recruits, "both lads and lassies go bare foot. . . . and for meals have rice water and rice and vegetable curries". Charles was so fired with enthusiasm at this news that he in turn read it at morning prayers in Shanghai. The zeal of those "Sally Army" candidates in India rubbed off on Priscilla. Inspired by their example, she redoubled her efforts to convert the British sailors in Shanghai.

On one occasion, the members of the team became so enthused that they jumped up on their chairs when Charles shouted during a service, "Stand on your chairs for Jesus!" while they were already standing on their feet singing the hymn, "Stand up for Jesus". Priscilla jumped with the rest! Only one missionary objected – but then it was not done for a Victorian lady missionary to show off a slender pair of ankles to the sailors of Her Majesty's fleet! However, Charles had already proved himself unconventional by giving up fame and fortune to wander round China as an itinerant evangelist so Priscilla's fervent ardour for souls would commend itself to him much more than the most correct behaviour according to books on etiquette.

Another visitor, calling at Shanghai on his way to Japan, was Charles' brother George. Charles, of course, made him very welcome, sharing his room at the Mission with him. Although aware that George had lost his zeal for the gospel, Charles wisely decided not to press him on the subject, and even went up to the Club to watch him play cricket. He had, though, shared his concern about George with the other evangelists before George had arrived so that many were praying for him.

This wiser strategy paid off. Within days, George could be found writing to his mother, "I can't tell you what peace and joy the Lord has given me in believing." He also confided in Charles, "If you'd tackled me about my faith when I first arrived and shared your room, I should have been off on that boat to Japan." Charles was becoming sensitive to the perfect timing and leading of the Holy Spirit in spite of his natural impetuosity to evangelise.

A real spirit of revival seemed to sweep through the murky streets of Shanghai, and with a marked improvement in health, Priscilla could be found singing hymns to popular secular tunes. "Why should the devil have all the best tunes?" must have been as much her concern as it is now. She could also be seen on her knees in drawing-rooms leading people to the Lord while Charles proved a popular caller on HMS Sapphire, where the Christians on board increased visibly in numbers.

In spite of their continuing private happiness and success in their mission, the time came for the trio to part. Priscilla travelled on her own, by steamer on the Yangtse, to central China whilst the two brothers set out north. Letters from Charles in Taiyuen-Fu sped frequently across the country to Priscilla in Ta-Ku-Tang where she had joined three other women. Priscilla's letters to Charles were all burnt according to her wishes later on so we can only guess the contents. It took four months of correspondence before she finally said "yes" to Charles' proposal of marriage.

Sufficient letters from Charles survive for readers to become aware that his devotion to Christ took precedence over his plans for their married life together. Charles was determined not to alter his lifestyle in the slightest to accommodate his future wife. They would continue to live simply, according to Chinese customs, and their wedding beforehand would avoid any lavish clothes or expensive banquet.

Priscilla was completely in agreement with him on these matters. When he presented her with the last £3,400 of the fortune he had inherited just before their marriage, she without hesitation decided to send every penny to a worthy cause. She was truly a woman after his own heart! She may have been tempted to keep a little back for their requirements but she quoted to her fiance the story of the rich young ruler, "We've got to do just that, Charles, sell all as the Lord said and start our married life obeying Him and living by faith."

And so it was that General Booth of the Salvation Army received a cheque for the final amount, together with a letter from Charles explaining his course of action. It speaks volumes about Charles and Priscilla. Their hearts were large enough to dispense with their last remaining capital, not even to their own mission but their sympathies went out world-wide to other deserving causes.

Naturally, Charles' letters to his mother contain many references to his beloved Priscilla. Mrs. Studd, curious about her future daughter-in-law, most likely found his descriptions exasperating. "I don't know her age . . .

and I haven't a photograph of her," Charles admitted. "Ask George, he'll give you more details."

Illness eventually delayed the date of their wedding. Charles himself had been ill for weeks and was nursed back to health by George. Priscilla contracted such a severe attack of pneumonia that her co-workers sent for Charles, afraid that she might not recover. He took charge of the situation.

Like everything else in Charles' life, the wedding celebrations were unusual and unconventional. To placate Pastor Shi, they went through a wedding ceremony with him officiating although he was an unlicensed preacher. Both bride and groom wore ordinary clothes and Charles even nodded off during the service, exhausted with his nursing duties! Afterwards they travelled down to Tientsin to go through a formal procedure with the Consul before they considered themselves fully man and wife.

Undoubtedly it was a love match. Again and again Charles commended the state of marriage in his letters, obviously heartily approving of it. "Marriage . . . is honourable and . . . out here it is especially good. There is a very great strength in loving and being loved . . . " But he was always aware of other relationships taking precedence in Christians' lives. "There is always a danger of marriage taking the razor edge off the passion for Jesus and souls." Yes, there is, but it never interfered with Charles' and Priscilla's love for the Lord. Their priorities were established right from the beginning.

# Chapter Seven

"He is no fool who gives what he cannot keep to gain what he cannot lose," wrote Jim Elliot when he was twenty-two. Seven years later, this twentieth century Christian, together with four other missionary friends, met their death at the hands of the savage Auca Indians in South America. He was called upon to make the final sacrifice.

God never demanded Charles and Priscilla to lay down their lives for His sake but they lived every day in the spirit of self-sacrifice. In addition to leaving behind fame, fortune and family, very pressing problems occupied them right from the beginning of their marriage. Particularly worrying were the political tensions that were becoming increasingly evident. People from other countries living in China were called "Foreign devils" and were not welcomed by the Chinese. They were often threatened and some lived in fear.

Three other lady workers accompanied the newlyweds to Lungang-Fu. First they were compelled to live in a house which was supposedly haunted and they met with a great deal of opposition and suspicion. If things went wrong in the city, the missionaries were held responsible almost automatically.

In spite of this, compensations could be found in the unlikely reactions of people who were exposed to the Christian gospel for the first time. Slides of the crucifixion scene made people break down in tears. When one notorious criminal realised that God was prepared to forgive even him, he went as an evangelist to the very place where his crimes had been committed. Although beaten and thrown into prison, this man insisted on preaching.

Drug-taking is not merely a modern dilemma, but has already existed for centuries. To the Studds it presented a formidable problem which they tried to combat. Opium addition was common in China at that time. The poor Chinese in their squalid opium dens were more to be pitied than blamed. With such a wretchedly poverty-stricken level of existence, opium appeared to be the only thing that could make them forget their miserable circumstances for a few short hours. However with the brief oblivion came their dependence on the drug which gradually possessed them. People doubted that the Christians could rid them of this terrifying addiction but the first two were cured in a month in the opium refuge which the Studds set up. Many hundreds passed through this place during the seven years it was open.

No wonder the Chinese regarded these "foreign devils" with suspicion at first. Their country had been virtually cut off from Western influence for centuries. Many of the country folk in the inland towns where they were working would probably never have met any non-Chinese before. Although culturally rich with a long tradition of civilisation behind it, China was also steeped in ignorance and superstition. Even Gladys Aylward, the famous missionary who worked amongst the Chinese nearly half a century later, still came up against many facets of this deep-rooted and mixed tradition. Because of previous social isolation from other countries, China accepted change very slowly.

One particularly cruel aspect of their traditions was to abandon unwanted baby girls at birth, leaving them to be prey for wild animals. This disturbed the Studds greatly and when, over the years, God gave them four little daughters, Charles believed that God had planned this so the Chinese would see how they loved them and cherished them. One boy was born to them after they returned to England but he only survived a couple of days. Priscilla lost another child at birth which affected her deeply. "I was broken-hearted", she wrote later, "but I made a covenant with God that I was not going to let sorrow . . . come into my life and ruin my life as a missionary." This was not callous and uncaring; in reality it represented an extremely costly sacrifice on the part of Priscilla. She wouldn't allow her own upset emotions and deep disappointment to interfere with their united service for the Lord.

Circumstances cannot have been easy for the Studds trying to bring up a family. Their only worldly goods at the start of their marriage were five dollars and some bedding. This bedding supply must have been absolutely essential as their first bed was made of bricks! True to his ideals, Charles never asked anyone for money, not even members of his own family. On many occasions, the larder was bare and Charles and his wife would get down on their knees to share the problem with God. Sometimes, almost miraculously, their needs were filled at the eleventh hour. But Charles never longed for security or the assurance of large reserve stocks of food or money. "Mother Hubbard's cupboard is safe; a full cupboard is very risky." He was a great admirer of George Müller of Bristol who prayed to God for funds to feed, clothe and house his orphan children and was sent over the years one and a half million pounds for that purpose, without making his needs known to any other human being. "Is not George Müller's God our God?" asked Charles rhetorically and somewhat indignantly.

It was only because Priscilla shared Charles' ideals that she was able to endure discomforts, hardships and even danger sometimes. The first severe test came when Priscilla's first baby was due. They had both agreed not to travel to the nearest doctor, as that would mean losing several weeks of missionary work. With merely the minimum nursing experience behind her, Priscilla had to act as her own midwife having for support her husband's practical help and Stanley Smith's prayers as he sat in the next room. Eventually a nurse arrived, but Priscilla started to deteriorate in health and it seemed she would not survive childbirth until Charles anointed her with oil and prayed over her.

For each of her five confinements, Priscilla managed without a doctor. The four girls were called Grace, Dorothy, Edith and Pauline. Stanley Smith came to the rescue again when one baby died at birth and he arrived to help with the burial. He was always a close friend and ready to give support and help in any crisis.

Next it was Charles' turn to suffer serious illness. His life was in the balance for a time and Priscilla prepared herself for the worst until Charles asked her to anoint him. She did so with the assistance of other faithful Chinese Christians and slowly he began to recover. They wondered if this was a signal to leave their missionary station in China. What message was God trying to put across to them? In spite of his weakness, Charles was convinced that God was not yet telling them to move on.

A year later, ten years after Charles had left England, the family prepared to leave China, obviously sure that this was God's timing for them. It must have been a wrench to say good-bye to their converts and the nurses who had helped with the family. The journey proved slow and treacherous, sometimes on foot, sometimes in sedan chairs borne by mules, sometimes on cargo boats on a river. Another complication was the war being waged with Japan and it didn't help that the English missionary family was sometimes mistaken for Japanese. Fortunately some of the children spoke Chinese which impressed the hostile crowds as they listened to the girls chattering in the local dialect.

After they boarded the steamer at Shanghai, the parents could at last, albeit partially, begin to relax. A long voyage home would give them an opportunity to unwind. Some of their responsibilities were over for the time being. To the four children, the wider world beyond their remote Chinese town must have appeared bewildering and yet exciting. And having arrived in England, life in London was vastly different for the four young missionary daughters. A city full of confusion and noise – with jostling crowds, bright lights, lavish displays in all the shop windows and roads full of carts, horse-buses and hansom cabs. They had never seen anything like it before. What a contrast to the narrow unpaved streets, of the small provincial town in China which had been their home for so many years!

Granny Studd welcomed the returning family with open arms. She wouldn't hear of them living with anyone else. So for the time being, the luxurious atmosphere of Hyde Park Gardens became their new environment. Generously, she also provided a nurse to look after the girls who was kept extremely busy with her lively and high spirited charges. None of them spoke English which didn't make matters any easier. Charles later told many amusing stories about his daughters' escapades in their early days in London.

The appointment of a nurse proved a necessity rather than a luxury. Both the parents came home with their health seriously affected by their unselfish service abroad. In time, Charles responded well to a slower pace of life and a more nourishing diet. Priscilla, however, showed little improvement and it became increasingly evident that she was unlikely to return to China. Fortunately, their financial needs were amply met by large cheques from supporters, which, although not making them affluent, ensured that they never lacked the basic necessities either then or later. God proved faithful to His obedient servants.

". . . there is absolutely no limit to what God can do with men or women who care not whether they live or die so long as they are allowed to fight for Christ and do the will of God." A man who believed that was unlikely to remain at home convalescing any longer than necessary. To begin with, Charles was content to take spasmodic speaking engagements in the British Isles and was soon rejoicing in new converts.

Soon he became aware of a much more distant call for help. Many years previously, just after the Cambridge Seven had set out for China, his brother Kynaston had made a tour of American universities at the evangelist Moody's invitation. His visit inspired and enthused the students to such an extent that the Student Volunteer Union was set up and later other organisations which became world-wide.

In 1896 Charles set off to retrace his brother's footsteps and stayed there eighteen months. There was no holding him back. Ignoring his own physical tiredness, he sometimes spoke at six meetings in one day. Even his leisure time was spent in counselling students and he travelled long distances between one speaking engagement and the next.

His letters graphically illustrate his involvement in both the larger gatherings and the one-to-one encounters. "Just caught a fish!" he exclaimed in Lincoln, Nebraska, indicating that he was following in the tradition of Peter who became, at the Lord's command, a fisher of men. Although the Studd brothers went their different ways in the world after leaving Cambridge, they were still extremely supportive of each other whenever from time to time their paths crossed. Mr. Weatherby little knew what a great service he was doing when he led each of the three Studd boys to faith in one day!

In his letters home, Charles gave many examples of students who turned to Christ as a result of his influence, but he wanted no credit for it. "To God be the glory!" was his constant call. On one occasion, he became quite incensed when people published complimentary articles about him and his work. "God can do little with those who love themselves or reputations," he wrote on another occasion. Indeed, it would have been easy to become elated by the success of his tour because the blessing spread like wildfire across the States. Without question, God was blessing Charles' efforts across the Atlantic.

# Chapter Eight

With such an enthusiastic response to the preaching of the Gospel in the United States, the temptation to stay and continue the tour was strong. Not that he wanted fame or fortune for himself, but it was gratifying to reap a rich harvest for Christ. Nevertheless Charles returned to England convinced that God was directing him that way. God had used him mightily several times on his long preaching tour and Charles had put all his mental and physical powers into it. "Let us no longer be passengers in the coaches of the Church but pushers of the war machine of God . . . till we . . . break the devil's line and destroy his last dug-outs . . . ", was a militant statement which clearly showed his attitude at that time.

But perhaps the most well-known and characteristic of his mottoes was found on a postcard on his desk, "If Jesus Christ be God and died for me, then no sacrifice can be too great for me to make for Him."

Yet however successful he may have become as an evangelist, some stronger force impelled him on as a pioneer; a trail-blazer in missionary endeavour. He was unique. No-one else could have taken on his role. God obviously chose him for a very special purpose to take the good news of Jesus to many parts of the world which had not heard the gospel. So China, America – where next?

It wasn't really a difficult decision. From early days

the Studd boys had been regaled with stories of India. Hadn't their father made his fortune there as a successful indigo planter? The family would never have enjoyed their life of ease, luxury and privilege without the money he had acquired in Tirhoot in Northern India. Edward Studd felt a responsibility to these people after his conversion and expressed a dying wish that one of his sons would take the message of the Gospel to that part of the world. For many years, it seemed as though this longing might never be fulfilled. Charles was away in China with his wife and daughters, but from time to time he recalled his father's solemn message. In a letter to his mother he remarked on the Indian people, "Are they not going to see Studd the ambassador of Jesus Christ?" He realised that all the name "Studd" meant to them was someone solely interested in amassing a large fortune through their work but not particularly concerned about their physical or spiritual welfare.

On his return to England, Charles found an unexpected ally in Mr. Vincent, his father's old friend who had been mainly responsible for Edward Studd's conversion. He, too, as a retired planter knew the situation in India well from first-hand experiences and was anxious for Edward's wishes to be carried out. Practically, he promised to take charge of all the preliminary arrangements if Charles were willing to make the journey out there. Promptly, Charles accepted the invitation and went out to Tirhoot for six months to investigate the possibilities of becoming an evangelist there.

While he was there, he held many meetings amongst the planters, men like his father who were bent on making their fortunes and then coming back home to retire and enjoy their wealth. There was nothing wrong in that – but it gave many of them rather a one-sided view of life. Financial success spurred them on. Money became the goal of the majority and once they had acquired sufficient they left India without thinking much about the poor native labourers who had worked hard to make them rich, with very scant reward for themselves. They felt little sense of responsibility for the working masses.

Charles made them aware both of their duties towards God and their fellow-men. He would remind them of Christ's saying in Matthew 6.19–20: "Lay not up for yourselves treasure on earth which moths and rust corrupt . . . but lay up for yourselves treasure in heaven." He might have spoken too of the rich fool in Luke, 12.16–21 who pulled down his store houses and built even greater only to be called suddenly to give account of himself to God after death: "Fool, this night your soul is required of you." Wealth in itself was not evil, it had enabled Edward and Charles to help a great many deserving Christian causes but it was not an end in itself.

Then, too, the planters were prompted to consider the needs of the Indians whose services they took very much for granted. "Who is my neighbour?" was a question Jesus compelled his followers to take seriously. Charles taught the planters to look at their Indian employees from a fresh viewpoint and regard them as fellow human beings with serious problems of poverty and neglect. Once the masters had become Christians, then that essential love and compassion would come flooding in for unfortunate men, women and children wherever they might be.

Those six months must have passed very quickly indeed with Charles packing a great deal of activity into a short space of time. Strangely enough though, it was not in Tirhoot that he was going to spend his six years in India. A call came from the Anglo-Indian Evangelisation Society to pastor an independent church in Ootacamund which he accepted and he remained there from 1900 – 1906.

Fortunately the climate and circumstances were favourable for Priscilla and the four girls to join him out there. During their formative years the girls were fortunate enough to enjoy the company of both their parents in China and India as well. Even though Charles travelled widely on his pastoral duties, he always returned home to base where Priscilla was "holding the fort" in his absence. Years lay ahead when he would be separated for long periods both from his wife and family – and he would be criticised and misunderstood for so doing. No-one, however, could take away from the girls the memories and influence of those years that the family was united. From their secure childhood years Charles' daughters derived strength, comfort and stability and his Christian training laid a solid basis for their lives.

Life was not all work and no play for Charles, however. With all his zeal for the gospel, he hadn't quite forgotten how to relax. Memories of his boyhood when he went out hunting, strapped to the saddle in his red jacket, must have stirred him when he introduced the girls to their first pony. This was a particularly lively one which pitched them all, one after the other, over his head as they tried to ride him. Priscilla saw danger and tried to stop the proceedings, but Charles insisted. "They've got to face up to fear. I want all my girls to have courage." Once they had overcome that obstacle he knew they would feel confident to mount almost any other horse.

While in India Charles found himself travelling extensively to reach the planters living in remote areas of Mysore and Madras. Communications then were as slow and difficult as he had already experienced in China. Temperatures rose to oppressive heights and roads were often only tracks or unrecognisable paths.

Other groups of people also claimed his attention. India in those days still belonged to the British Empire so large numbers of soldiers could always be found in the barracks, often homesick or at least glad to talk with a fellow-Englishman. Higher up the social scale, officers and their wives welcomed him, as did government officials and the Governor of Madras, Lord Ampthill, a fellow-Etonian.

A cool hill station away from the burning heat of the plains of India was the ideal place for a hectic social whirl which many British people in India enjoyed. Charles found that a full programme of events had been arranged every hot season as middle and upper class Britishers flocked to the hills to avoid the discomfort of the scorching plains. It was a constant struggle to interest such people in the claims of Christ upon their lives when the pull of worldly society dragged them in the opposite direction. (Mother Teresa, many years later, during her first term of service in India, met the same problem.) Life in a hill station offered so much amusement and enjoyment that people lived only for the present and were unwilling to consider more serious questions. In spite of this, Priscilla claimed that Charles usually witnessed one or two conversions every week.

Because of his background, Charles felt quite at home in Government House and was particularly grateful when the Ampthills invited him and Priscilla to stay when he was suffering an extremely bad attack of asthma, even arranging medical treatment for him. This asthma was to prove a constant scourge over the years and we find him writing once, ". . . my lungs were choked up with asthma and I cried, 'How long, Lord? . . . I longed for rest and peace . . . but He laid hold of me and comforted me awhile.'" This was no new experience in India. Charles had been an asthmatic for some years and it often meant that he only slept for about a couple of hours every night, often sitting up in a chair, gasping for breath. Modern drugs which now alleviate this condition were not available at the turn of the century.

In view of his poor health, it seems incredible that Charles joined a cricket tour so he could have more personal contact with soldiers playing in the regimental teams. In 1904 he made two double centuries, which were all the more amazing because he had been out of practice for some years. Charles was like Kipling's ideal man who ". . . could walk with kings nor lose the common touch". Lord Kitchener and Lord Curzon the Viceroy chatted to him during visits to Ootacamund. People respected him for his sporting achievements and his unashamed profession of the Christian faith. His name still stood for a magnificent cricketing record which up to that time had never been beaten in the game.

"Preacher's kids" as they are commonly called, often have a difficult life. They have a narrow tight-rope to walk. People expected them to conform to a certain type of behaviour by that age. But probably because of their close, happy family unit, all the four girls independently made decisions to follow Christ during their years in India. Characteristically, Charles baptised the girls himself, even digging out a large pond in the garden which houseboys filled with kettles of warm water because the day was cold. Among the guests and friends of the family at the service was Amy Carmichael, herself a pioneer missionary in India. Afterwards the girls teased their father that he had muddled them up and two had been baptised under the wrong names! Edith wrote about it light-heartedly in her journal, describing the girls clad in nightdresses, hardly more damp than the congregation, crowding under umbrellas in the pouring rain round the baptismal tank. But it left a deep impression on her in later years although the occasion was touched with humour.

Edith went on to describe those years as "our happiest childhood". Conditions cannot have been nearly as primitive as they experienced in China. They received many invitations to picnics, badminton parties and all kinds of social occasions at Government House. The girls never lacked an escort for any of these functions. Young officers from the regiments abounded and proved only too willing to accompany them. Sometimes Charles himself took his daughters out in a buggy cart with "Billy the Waler" harnessed in front. Priscilla would greet them with profound relief on their return, knowing they had been rattling madly up and down steep hills and narrow tracks.

Midnight feasts in their bedroom with food smuggled in from parties took place from time to time. But, as Edith admitted, "We had nearly driven three governesses nuts", and at last the moment came for these young ladies to acquire more book knowledge and social graces as well.

# Chapter Nine

The Studd family returned to England once more in 1906. What would be their pattern of service in the future? Charles himself was aptly described as "a museum of diseases". He could well have been excused for taking life easy from that time on. Priscilla, too, having been compelled to leave China years previously because of her ill-health had certainly had never been robust since.

One major problem became solved almost immediately upon their return. The girls had reached a stage in their education where their needs could no longer be met at Ootacamund. Ideally, their parents wished to send them to boarding school in England but that entailed a great deal of money which they simply did not possess. However, owing to the kindness of a relative, the three older girls were sent to Lausanne to a finishing school for eighteen months. The days dragged slowly by. Strangely enough, the girls who had survived happily in China and India, felt homesick in Switzerland without their parents and longed for the familiar sounds and sights of life at Granny's house in London.

On their re-appearance, having acquired no great fluency in French in the process, the three older girls were again parcelled off, this time to Sherborne School. Yet they seemed to gain little from formal education in spite of being intelligent and well-travelled. The schools said that they had suffered from "too many governesses" and the trio were quite relieved to be done with school and to participate for a change in the delights of the London season.

Now nearly twenty-one years had elapsed since the "Cambridge Seven" had set out for China with their names ringing in everyone's ears. Public memory is notoriously fickle. Would people have forgotten Charles Studd and his brilliant athletic career which he abandoned to work as a missionary? Perhaps, but over the next couple of years, Charles found himself in constant demand as a preacher for meetings and Church services. Most likely many from his congregations were far from regular church-goers but flocked to hear him because they admired the man and his achievements. Charles did not speak in religious cliches and pious platitudes. Occasional flashes of humour lightened his sermons and his language was down-to-earth and free from class-consciousness. By this means he won over many people who previously had little sympathy for him and his message.

"The telling of the simple gospel – Christ Himself – carries with it its own reward of the joy unspeakable that Peter wrote about." Perhaps it is wrong to speak about Charles preparing a sermon because a further quote from *Fool and Fanatic* reads, "Don't go into the study to prepare a sermon . . . go there to go to God and get so fiery that your tongue is like a burning coal and you have got to speak." Charles spoke from divinely-inspired compulsion. Far from letting his platform appearances become an ego-trip to boost himself, Charles lost no time in describing his own personal encounter with Christ. First he told of his nominal Christian behaviour before God sent him out for service – correct and formal outwardly, but lifeless within. Then, "Words became deeds, the commands of Christ . . . battle calls to be obeyed." At this stage, some of his enthusiasm rubbed off on his hearers and they began to covet this experience for themselves. Dull, formal religion might hold little attraction but this new sort of Christianity sounded exciting and adventurous. Might it not be worth trying for a change?

So for about two years Charles enjoyed an itinerant ministry, preaching more or less wherever he was invited. Possibly some thought that the Studds were settling down to a normal family life at last. After ten years in China and then six in India, no-one could blame them for wanting to stay at home. At the back of his mind, Charles was still toying with the idea of returning to India but he had made no definite decision when one day in Liverpool he saw a humorous notice which changed the direction of his life completely.

"Cannibals want missionaries," read the placard and it so tickled Charles that he felt compelled to go in the building it was posted outside and investigate. It was no ordinary man that he met there. Dr. Karl Kumm had walked across Africa and wanted to share his experiences with other people. Just after the turn of the century that was a very courageous enterprise. Roads in many areas were non-existent and everywhere the vegetation much more dense and prolific. Few modern means of communication existed but Karl had shown great determination and persistence. "Many other people had visited there before me," he told Charles, "trading parties, big-game hunters, government officials and scientists. Yet, imagine it, no Christian had ventured there solely to preach the gospel."

This remark hit Charles hard. Well, he couldn't go, could he? "I've no money, my health is far from good. Tropical Africa would be impossible for me," he kept telling himself, but all the time he had a feeling that God was urging him on. Karl wanted the two of them to cross the continent again together but Charles fell ill with malaria and the scheme had to be abandoned. Next, a group of business men promised to back him on a trip to Southern Sudan, a thousand miles south of Khartoum, subject to a favourable medical report. The doctor vetoed this so again, nothing happened.

At least the committee were willing for him to make the journey to Khartoum, but no further, on the doctor's advice. Believing that they had his good at heart, they withdrew the funds when Charles refused to give any undertaking that he would limit his journey. Where did all this leave him? Without money, declared unfit by the doctor and let down by his group of sponsors, Charles felt he must rely completely on God. "I will blaze a trail – even if I die in the attempt", summed up his determination to go to Khartoum and beyond, into the heart of Africa.

He made his own plans and three weeks only remained to him to collect sufficient money for the trip and make all his final preparations. Undeterred, he turned up in Birmingham the next day to address a meeting as arranged. He let no-one know of his ambitious plans but held an inner conviction that God would supply all his needs. Next Charles travelled on to Liverpool for weekend speaking engagements. It was only as he was leaving that a well-wisher pressed £10 into his hand – hardly a large sum but it gave Charles enough encouragement to make a detour to the docks to put the money down as a deposit for his passage to Port Said. His faith was rewarded. Sufficient funds came in for him to sail. "The best cure for discouragement or qualms is another daring plunge of faith", was one of his sayings and it was certainly appropriate at this point in his life.

So at fifty-one and with poor health, he sailed without even the approval of his own wife. Many people thought he was wrong to go, but on the first night in his cabin

God gave him a remarkable assurance. "This trip is not only for the Sudan, it is for the whole unevangelised world." Charles believed this promise immediately, and it strengthened him to answer his many critics. He firmly believed he was obeying God's call to Africa.

It would have been impossible to foresee that Charles' sailing was to give rise to the growth of a remarkable world-wide missionary movement now called the World Evangelisation Crusade. In 1913, Charles' aims were ". . . evangelising the unevangelised world in the shortest possible time, starting with the heart of Africa". Now, over seventy years later the WEC has nine hundred missionaries in over forty countries, with five hundred more associated with Christian Literature Crusade which spreads the gospel literature and Christian books.

But on December 15th, 1910, the only visible evidence was one solitary middle-aged man in poor health boarding a boat at Liverpool with no companion and no support at home. Stirred by the message given to him by God on the first night, he poured out his soul in burning, emotional letters home to his wife. Saddened by their parting, he wrote to reassure her of God's love and support and also to cheer and encourage her. All the physical effort and bodily weakness he had experienced had been a preparation for this new work to come, he was convinced.

"Think of the heart of Africa, and you are in heaven on earth in a jiffy," he wrote cheerfully. Not only was Charles sure that God was pouring health and strength into him, but he felt positive that Priscilla's health would also improve, she would become a great soul-winner for Christ and all their four daughters would be "white-hot Christian warriors". An even greater revival than that at Shanghai was going to take place, he was sure. Although Priscilla remained in England, he always visualised his work as a joint effort, "You and I will do it – do it for Jesus."

Charles was held up at Khartoum for several weeks, but, being the man he was, he found plenty of activities to fill up the time. He both preached in the English church and held a mission among the Northumberland Fusiliers stationed there. The authorities approved of his work and he was invited to the palace of the English ruler, Sir Reginald Wingate, for several dinner parties. Perhaps it was just as well that this enforced delay took place because it gave Charles a chance to recover from the voyage and plan his strategy for the future.

Eventually he set off for Southern Sudan with Bishop Gwynne as his companion. There they were joined by Archdeacon Shaw of the Church Missionary Society. This indomitable trio spent two and a half months jouneying through the Bahr-el-Ghazal. Conditions were hardly ideal, particularly for someone with Charles' medical history. Malaria was rampant and the poor roads subject to flooding in the rainy season. Even a severe attack of malaria after his return to Khartoum did not cause Charles to swerve from his appointed path. He said, ". . . a missionary ought to be a fanatic or he encumbers the ground".

However, in spite of his natural enthusiasm, Charles did not act impetuously. It was evident that the CMS work already established in that area could cope quite adequately with the sparse population. So it seemed pointless to spend resources and energy there when the rest of the unevangelised world beckoned.

God had not stirred Charles to leave home and risk poverty merely to be halted in his tracks when he arrived in the Sudan. Charles received more information which he interpreted as a direct message from God that his future work lay beyond in what was then known as Belgian Congo amongst needy people who knew nothing of the Christian gospel. The call from God could not be mistaken. "Dare you go back to England . . . knowing of these masses who have never heard of Jesus Christ?"

Writing to his mother later when she urged him to return to England and seek a well-paid position there, he put the question to her, "Could you imagine Paul leaving his work to go and seek some lucrative employment in Jerusalem or Rome? Well . . . I could not do such a thing." No doubt his thinking had been influenced for years by Hudson Taylor who first stirred him to join the missionary enterprise in China. "I refuse to be discouraged," said Hudson once, "I will praise the Lord." This is certainly characteristic of Charles' attitude in the many crises which befell him.

Far from deterred by the enormity of this new mission field, Charles returned to England to build up enthusiasm for his Heart of Africa Mission. Naturally, in selecting places in which he could explain his future plans, he made sure that Cambridge, from whence the Seven had originally set out, was included. Many young men from the Inter-Collegiate Christian Union received a distinct missionary call as a result of his visit which affected the rest of their lives.

Somehow Charles also found time to write several booklets – among them *The Chocolate Soldier*, containing an impassioned appeal for volunteers to join in with the evangelisation of the vast continent of Africa. He reckoned that five hundred millions had yet to be reached with the gospel. With the development of modern technology the means of communication were becoming easier.

He spelt out the basic principles of the new crusade. They underlined the necessity of absolute faith in God, belief in the Scriptures and obedience to God's command. Again he emphasised that no financial appeals should be made. His workers should rely on God alone for their supplies. So anyone signing up as one of his helpers would need to be tough, determined and dedicated. How many young people would respond to such a challenge?

# Chapter Ten

One factor that made the parting for Africa easier this second time was that Charles left British shores with Priscilla's blessing. It wasn't an easy decision but God made it clear to her through her own personal Bible readings that He would remove all her fears of her husband being seven thousand miles away. He wouldn't change the circumstances necessarily but He would ensure peace of mind for Priscilla throughout.

In an affectionate letter home to Priscilla, Charles stated, "Truly this has been like the Seven going out. Goodbye my darling Priscilla." This note of confidence and triumph persisted in other letters to friends. "We have a multi-millionaire to back us up . . . He gave me a cheque-book free and urged me to draw upon him."

One person only accompanied Charles on this new trip: Alfred Buxton, the son of his old friend the Rev. Barclay F. Buxton. Alfred, not yet twenty-one had cut short his medical studies at Cambridge to take part in this trek. It was he who would marry Edith, the Studd's third daughter, later on but for the moment his thoughts and preoccupations were with crossing the difficult terrain safely. They travelled through Kenya and Uganda to the shores of Lake Albert. Their journey was like that of Christian's in Bunyan's well-known *Pilgrim's Progress*, "We had not passed this way before; many were the difficulties and obstacles in our path." Their combined lack of French made it tricky conversing with Belgian officials. Alfred succumbed to a serious attack of fever, which was not surprising in such conditions, and it took him a week to recover. What was even more alarming, Alfred received a cable from his relatives urging him to give up the project and return home. He must have been under a considerable amount of pressure. However, in spite of these and other problems including a fire in camp, the two pressed on and Alfred was kept free from further attacks of fever.

They were surprised, and delighted, to receive a welcome into the Congo by the Belgians. Mosquitoes, fierce animals and savage tribes all impeded their progress somewhat, but they went on their way undaunted. Charles' letters home contain humorous accounts of many experiences, including an encounter with cannibals. Next it was Charles' turn to go down with fever. In desperation, Alfred anointed him with the only oil available – kerosene – but effectual healing took place.

A first batch of letters from England brought the welcome news that Charles' first grandchild, Ann, had arrived safely to his daughter Dorothy.

After the Congo, they were treading in the footsteps of Stanley, the great explorer, through the huge Ituri forest lands. The going was heavy and dangerous. At one time they were halted altogether through lack of porters. Even natives who knew the area well were not keen to travel further. Yet eventually they reached Niangara, the heart of Africa, after being on the road for nine months. To their relief, it seemed an ideal base for their operations being fairly close to large centres of population. October 16th, 1913, was the date when the two intrepid travellers arrived at their destination.

Originally they had planned an alternative base, but

they felt God had led them in that direction. It was a better location than they had hoped for with good soil and more population groups within reach. Charles applied for a site at Nala from the Government, five days' journey south and almost at the same time the Chief gave his permission for a settlement at Niangara. In this way, the first two mission stations were started almost simultaneously which involved a great deal of hard manual work: tree felling and forest clearing.

Building also became a top priority. Charles and Alfred had travelled for nine months, sometimes on foot, sometimes on their bicycles when the terrain allowed it. Through thick forests they had trudged, feeding on bananas, bread and tea and living in tents. So as soon as the land became available at Niangara they built a large mud and wattle house for the magnificent sum of £6. It seemed so luxurious after living in tents for so long that they nick-named it Buckingham Palace.

But they didn't allow themselves to rest there for long. After a short time, they set off south for Nala to fix the boundaries for the new station. Passing through territory that had belonged to warring cannibal tribes only ten years previously, they were received in a friendly fashion and many converts were made. The hearts of the tribes-people appeared receptive to the Christian gospel. Charles and Alfred did not stop short at the message of salvation. They taught their hearers that Christianity made a difference to every day life as well. It wasn't just a question of church attendance but living peacefully with neighbours and behaving fairly and considerately towards everyone.

Charles' health suffered. He was dogged by neuralgia on that trip, which caused splitting headaches at times, but they were counterbalanced by the joy he experienced in ministering to the people to whom God had sent him. His sense of humour saved the day on many occasions, too. In describing the way they made progress across difficult country, he commented, ". . . one young lady held my hand one side pulling me up a gulley, and another elder one did ditto the other side; one even put her arm around my neck!" He wrote amusing descriptions of peoples' amazement at their first sight of men on bicycles. "Here is our 'Eldorado'," he stated, confident that they had reached their objective.

Two more treks were undertaken to Poko and Bambili, ensuring that four centres for the work were fixed in only two years. Heartening news reached them of five more workers on their way out from England. At this juncture, Charles and Alfred felt it right to separate for a while. Alfred was to make Nala his base, to look after the new arrivals and to continue with his Bible translation work. He also had the joy of baptising the first twelve converts there, men whose lives had been turned inside out by the message of the gospel. Later Alfred's language study resulted in translations of the New Testament and half the Old Testament in the main language of the area. But this took some years to accomplish.

Meanwhile Charles struggled on a thousand mile journey to the mouth of the Congo where he boarded ship for England. In spite of all the dangers and problems he encountered on this long trip, the worst news to reach him was that his wife had been taken severely ill. The doctor advised the life of an invalid for her from that time. In future all her activities would be very restricted. Priscilla observed these instructions meticulously at first, although she found it difficult because she too now recognised that God had called both her and her husband to pioneer this new crusade, and wished to play an energetic part in the work.

From her sick bed, however, she formed prayer groups and sent out copies of the Heart of Africa magazine, helped by her daughters Edith and Pauline. The other two girls were already married but Grace's husband, Martin Sutton, also gave his assistance until his early death. Much to Charles' surprise when he landed in England, he found a Mission Headquarters already established.

Originally, he had bought a family house in Norwood, South London for £200. Charles had furnished it economically, attending auctions and picking up pieces of furniture and rolls of carpet at bargain prices. Of course, as the years rolled on and the Mission grew, number 17 Highland Road was bursting at the seams with extra guests, missionary candidates and piles of literature. The next step in faith was to rent the garage next door for storage and then eventually Priscilla took over the whole of the house, number 19, as well. But all that lay ahead in the future. When Charles arrived home he was overjoyed to find number 17 a hive of activity.

But Charles was not interested in remaining at home to rest, neither did Priscilla demand that Charles stayed by her bedside. They agreed that Charles should set off, travelling for nine months up and down the country, raising support for the mission and recruiting new candidates.

Conditions weren't easy. It was 1915, and the country was plunged in the First World War with all its suffering, heartache and losses. Charles was subject to constant attacks of malaria. He felt the bitter cold of an English winter after the tropical temperatures in Africa. But nothing deterred him. Writing to a friend he commented, "Oh these train journeys. So slow and so cold, but God is always there."

In between meetings, Charles wrote impassioned appeals for the missionary magazine. It horrified him that young men preferred to stay at home preaching to "Britain's 40 million evangelised inhabitants" rather than "fighting at the front among 1,200 million heathen." "I blush for shame at the thought of all this work commanded to be done, and think of the thousands of young men at home who say they love Christ, yet like Saul's army run and hide when Goliath appears." Words poured off his pen as eloquently and vehemently as from his lips. So overpowering was his conviction that he was unable to recognise obstacles in anyone else's way.

By July 1916, Charles assembled a small party of eight to return with him to Africa. Among them was his daughter Edith, going out to marry Alfred. In her life-story, *Reluctant Missionary*, she confessed, ". . . I can remember kissing Mother quickly and flying . . . from the house for fear of crying." One can understand her doubts and hesitations. Although she loved Alfred, she hadn't seen him for years and was leaving a comfortable existence in London for an unknown future in the African bush.

The others appeared equally unsure of what lay ahead. On board ship, Charles collected them together each day and tried to train them for their new responsibilities. He also gave a series of Bible studies on outstanding biblical characters daily throughout the voyage. The atmosphere never became holiday-like. It was still war time. Constant danger from enemy torpedoes threatened them, and all the port-holes were blacked out. Everyone was relieved when the three week voyage finished and the party could land on the shores of Africa. Even then, another thousand miles had to be covered – 700 miles up the Congo on a river steamer and then a 300 mile footslog through the forest. The complete journey lasted four months, but Alfred met them partly along the way, to encourage them in the last stage of it.

Charles described their arrival at Nala as being "like a Lord Mayor's Show". He and his companions were delighted to see the transformation in the village. Rows of mud and thatch houses stood in tidy avenues lined by palm trees, together with a church and a school house. Alfred alone could take the credit for this. After an absence of two years, the native Christians kept telling themselves, "Bwana won't come back." Yet return he did, so they put on a procession with musical instruments followed by a luscious feast under the trees to celebrate.

Charles needed but three weeks to recover from his long journey and then he had to pack up his equipment once more to accompany Edith and Alfred to Niangara where Belgian officials were waiting to perform the wedding ceremony.

The evening before the wedding found the bride-to-be colouring her white shoes with a weak solution of tea so they would match her cream dress. She admitted that her bridegroom's trousers were a "little short and his sleeves a trifle long" and his shirt collar was held in place at the back with a safety pin, but all went well in spite of it being the first "white" wedding in the heart of Africa. There was no precedent to follow, no ritual pattern. Belgian officials only took five minutes over signing the necessary papers and then cups of tea and wedding cake were handed round, perhaps rather incongruously.

Certainly, Charles was fortunate in having such a family. Some of his enthusiasm had obviously rubbed off on to them. His daughter Edith had already joined him in the Congo and had married his close companion. Later, Pauline would travel out there too to work with her husband, Norman Grubb, on the mission station. At home his wife put all her efforts into establishing a home base for the Heart of Africa campaign, with a great deal of assistance from her son-in-law Martin Sutton. The girls could have turned their backs on the discomforts of missionary work completely, having been educated in Switzerland and later at Sherborne. From their grandmother's house in Hyde Park Gardens, they moved in the upper echelons of society in a world peopled by nannies, butlers and copious supplies of manservants and housemaids. With this background, they could have craved a completely different lifestyle. Often they felt pulled in two directions. Edith admitted in her book ". . . only half of me belonged to the life of Hyde Park Gardens, the other half felt guilty I did not follow my parents . . . secretly I felt at war with myself."

Back in Africa there was no time for a long honeymoon for Edith and Alfred, the pressures and urgency of the work being too great. One significant phrase in a letter from Charles in April, 1917, sums it all up. "The work here is a marvel . . . the finger of God is here."

# Chapter Eleven

Edith was soon to find out that her father preferred to live like the locals in whatever country he found himself rather than impose European customs on foreign peoples. This started from his early days in China when he adopted the Chinese thick padded clothing. In Africa he ate the food of the country apart from an occasional treat like a cup of tea. "Father . . . said as long as . . . missionaries travelled first class, lived out of tins, ate bread and butter and drank tea, the world would never be evangelised," was Edith's comment. At least she had her own way about furniture and local carpenters knocked up chairs, tables, beds and shelves out of planks of wood. Charles maintained his spartan way of life to the end only using simple camp furniture. Alfred and Edith tried to strike a happy medium in making life a little easier and more comfortable for themselves and yet not antagonising the Africans. Charles didn't think it wise to enjoy a much higher standard of living than the natives.

Many encouragements spurred him on. Chiefs were beginning to build schools and houses to attract the missionaries to work in their territory. After only two and a half years, a hundred black people had been converted and baptised. Even more thrilling, about twenty African Christians offered to go out and evangelise the villages around Nala. Later, more volunteers came forward. Like Jesus when He sent out seventy disciples for a similar purpose in Luke 10 Charles gave them practical advice, rule number one being "If you don't want to meet the devil during the day, meet Jesus before dawn!"

Charles believed in close contact with the Africans at all times, "The closer you live to these natives the better," he maintained. He allowed them the freedom of his house and verandah. Edith found it more difficult to practice such open-hearted hospitality at first, particularly when a stray man from a neighbouring mission turned up for breakfast on the first morning of their honeymoon!

Charles' sense of humour bubbles up in some of the accounts of his expeditions in his letters. He related once how a native carrier, having first carried his bicycle across a stream, came back for Charles and then somehow managed to stumble with him into the water. On another occasion a tin of treacle got mixed up with his books, papers and clothes and the sticky mess had to be washed by hand from every sheet of paper.

There was a choice of over ninety translated hymns to sing at their church services – "all jolly fine stuff" boasted Charles, happily. Another way of getting the gospel message across was to put a slide show on in the evenings. This was a great novelty to the Africans. A third mission station was opened, this time leading into the Ituri Province at Deti. Mr. and Mrs. Ellis, the missionaries who first went to open up the work showed tremendous personal courage because the Chief had been a cannibal. Charles was thrilled when he travelled there and preached in the "Worship Shed". This grass hut was packed to capacity. It took Charles several minutes just to work his way to the front, picking his way across the crowded floor. Also boys' and girls' boarding schools were started in Nala.

In spite of the many encouragements, some drawbacks arose. Charles' health, for instance, created a source of anxiety from time to time and Edith and Alfred nursed him tenderly through many bouts of sickness. Next, Charles had to say goodbye to his daughter and son-in-law and their new baby daughter, Susan, while they went on furlough, together with four others. This left the number of missionaries on the field perilously low. Wartime conditions had stopped reinforcements joining them.

Charles generously praised Alfred for all his devotion over three years. "To Alfred's nursing and care I . . . owe my life . . . truly no mother ever nursed her child more tenderly and efficiently." A farewell meeting took place in Nala before the Buxton family set off for Europe.

After the growth and success of the early years, the next period proved to be a time of severe testing. Only six white missionaries remained, thinly spread out over the whole area. It didn't help that Charles was suffering with ulcers on his legs and a maddening skin irritation on all his limbs. Yet it wasn't the physical pain that worried him so much but the disappointments that some of his new converts caused him, but they were inexperienced Christians, and had much to learn.

There were compensations. Charles became particularly heartened by the numbers of native Christians who attended his early prayer meeting at five o'clock in the morning. He called their prayers "red-hot shots from their very hearts", finding their naive, informal requests to God much more real than those expressed in formal prayers. They prayed over him and for him, causing him to write in a letter home, ". . . I think it is just the prayers of these people (and of course you all at home) that keeps me alive."

However much Charles disliked disappointments, he knew only too well that like his hero, the apostle Paul, it was necessary for him to undergo trials at times. "Paul . . . realised . . . suffering brought instant joy to his soul from God, which totally obliterated the pain." In another letter he wrote, "A man is not known by his effervescence but by the amount of real suffering he can stand."

Like a beleagured garrison, the stalwart six carried on the work in the heart of Africa until reinforcements finally arrived in 1920. Amongst the party were Pauline and her husband Norman Grubb. The journey even in those days took three months by ship, train and river boat to Khartoum, then on a river steamer up the Nile. After that came a hundred miles by truck and the last three hundred miles were completed on foot and by bike. Norman had never met his father-in-law before so felt a little apprehensive. Charles gave them a loving welcome but soon Norman and Pauline were in for a shock. Just because they were relatives, they were accorded no special treatment. Charles didn't believe in favouritism. Norman confessed later in his book, *Once Caught, No Escape*, they had thought "they were bringing help and refreshment to the tired little band in Congo" but the six, far from being full of gratitude to the new recruits, merely expected them to stand shoulder to shoulder with them in the fight.

Charles didn't take too kindly to suggestions and criticisms from anyone, particularly inexperienced personnel, but he wisely sent Pauline and Norman off to Deti to run the new station on their own. Much good work was carried out there. A few mistakes were made but Norman and Pauline had the grace to humble themselves and openly admit their failings. Local Christians and the rest of the European team working out in Congo lovingly forgave them and they were restored in close, happy fellowship. They carried on working selflessly until 1923 when they were forced to return home because of Pauline's health. Sadly, their first baby, a boy called Noel, had died in Africa on his first birthday.

Fortunately, other reinforcements kept arriving until the original six were increased to nearly forty in three years. Alfred and Edith returned in 1921, leaving Susan and her new brother Lionel behind in England with Alfred's parents. Again, poor Edith was faced with another traumatic parting. "We hurried through the farewell and ran down the stairs," she wrote, recalling the previous occasion when she had left her mother and sisters behind to marry Alfred in Africa.

Once more, Charles felt free to branch out as a pioneer missionary into new territory with the existing stations well-manned. A big centre of population existed at Ibambi, four days journey from Nala. It was in this direction that Charles decided to move and he set up his headquarters there in 1922. Soon the white "Bwana" became well-known in that area also and calls for help and teaching came in from all over the region. At first people trekked to Ibambi to receive teaching and then baptism. When he had taught the initial converts, Charles began to visit other settlements.

No one could mistake Bwana coming along the trail. By now, his tall figure had begun to stoop a little. In his cotton jacket and shorts his frame looked gaunt. A bushy beard jutted out from his chin and his skin was weather-beaten and sunburnt from long exposure to tropical temperatures. Constantly he was under pressure from people to take a long furlough. He was worn out with his life-time's work and everyone thought he needed a rest. To them came this reply, "Bwana . . . going home . . . where there are churches and chapels and mission-rooms galore and . . . leave your people to rush headlong into hell?" Only someone as single-minded as Charles could act with such dedication.

Pauline remained in England until the 1930s but

Norman returned to the Congo. The decision can't have been easy but both felt it would give more stability to their children born in England, Paul and Priscilla, if their mother remained with them. Alfred and Edith stayed in Africa until 1925, but Charles urged them to return after Alfred was taken seriously ill. This illness never completely left him although he nobly struggled on in various forms of Christian service.

Charles spoke of himself as one who had been called "fool and fanatic again and again". He certainly didn't consider himself indispensable but only claimed to be filling a "yawning gap". Strangely enough, Priscilla at home gained strength after her life had almost been despaired of. She threw herself into work for the mission with renewed fervour after Charles left for Africa. Rising from her sick-bed, she became full of energy and enthusiasm.

Dorothy's husband, Gilbert Barclay, joined her in the work in 1919 on the understanding that the crusade became world-wide. Pioneers went out to start evangelising the Amazon basin. The going was extremely tough and one missionary even lost his life. Another spearhead thrust into Central Asia, which was again difficult territory. Converting Moslems always means slow progress. Nevertheless, fruitful contacts were made and WEC amalgamated with the Central Asian Mission to strengthen the Christian effort in that area. After initial failure, centres were established in Arabia and West Africa.

Charles refused to be drawn off to head new enterprises. Instead he soldiered on, building on the foundations already laid down in Congo. All teams from WEC obeyed without questioning Charles' primary rule that no appeals should be made for money. And God honoured their faith, enough coming in by way of unsolicited funds to keep the mission completely free from debt.

Charles was never happy with superficial Christianity. The standards he set took a great deal of attaining – they were too high some people found. It would have been easier to remain content with more of a surface show of faith but that wasn't Charles' way. "I am getting . . . fearful lest fizz and froth take the place of the Divine fire among us." In upholding this point of view, he created opposition and problems but he refused to be satisfied with second best.

Another decision which he made became justified later on and that was to use the trade language called Bangala. This did away for the necessity to learn and understand the many tribal languages which would have taken years to accomplish. It greatly speeded up the translation work.

Not only was Charles concerned about the personal holiness of his African converts he also became disturbed about the way in which European workers resented the austerity of their daily life, the lack of any luxury and opportunities for leisure. Charles refused to compromise and in so doing even upset some of the mission's committee at home. He felt the criticisms and misunder-standings deeply but was only prepared to change if God pointed him in another direction.

It almost seemed as though deadlock had been reached until one night in 1925 a breakthrough was achieved. The occasion started off as just an ordinary prayer meeting at Ibambi where Charles met with eight other missionaries. He spoke from Hebrews 11, the roll-call of the heroes of faith and suddenly flashpoint occurred. One after another the missionaries stood up and rededi-cated their lives in complete surrender to God.

The enthusiasm engendered spread throughout the mission stations and Charles had the satisfaction of knowing in the last few years of his life that true progress was being made. "The work is reaching a sure foundation at last and now we will go bounding forward." This renewal was not just peculiar to white missionaries but touched the lives of hundreds of black Christians also. It is all the more remarkable because these were first-generation Christians who, before Charles' arrival in the Congo, had been cannibals, thieves, murderers, involved in witchcraft and many occult practices. Their new faith was so different from their old religion and the white man's culture so opposed to their own. At least Charles tried to keep his life-style as simple as possible with a minimum of possessions so he could identify closely with them. In him they saw someone who not only preached but practised his beliefs.

# Chapter Twelve

In these last few years, the remaining threads in the colourful tapestry of Charles' life were being interwoven. From aristocratic home in Victorian England to hovels in remote areas of China, from a pastorate in India to pioneer trail-blazing in uncivilised Africa, Charles drew a rich store of experiences which helped to mould the pattern of his thinking and his behaviour.

Unfortunately a rift had occurred between Charles and his son-in-law Alfred Buxton which meant that Alfred sought other areas to evangelise rather than rejoin Charles in the Congo. He worked selflessly and tirelessly in Ethiopia until forced to flee by the Italian invasion of the country. Finally he was killed in a London blitz in 1940, after three years' efforts in England to have the bible of Emperor Haile Selassie published. This precious document, translated into Amharic (the language of the common people) by monks and priests of the Coptic Church, was placed in Alfred's hands by the Emperor himself and smuggled out of the country.

It was a great pity that this misunderstanding arose between Charles and Alfred but even that situation was used by God for good. Alfred's labours in Ethiopia covered essential, urgent work that had to be accomplished before war closed many doors to the gospel in that country. Edith commented in her book that when the two first sailed for Africa in 1913, people said of them "One is too old, and the other too young." Charles himself dubbed them, "Balaam's ass and Noah's dove". That these two were forced to separate after many years of comradeship caused heartaches in the family but in retrospect Edith wrote, "God . . . seemed to bring good out of evil, enabling them to fulfil the work . . . each felt He had given them to do; even by their diversity making the Gospel go further round the world."

Difficulties arose too about the problem of who should succeed Charles as field leader. He was the first to admit his frail mortality. Already a victim of many debilitating diseases, he considered it essential to train someone specifically suited for that role while he still had the time and energy to groom a younger man. Norman Grubb hoped it would be himself, and was deeply disappointed when Charles chose instead Jack Harrison, a mission worker from the poorest slums of Liverpool, a contrast to Charles' own privileged background. However, in the end Norman was able to accept that decision without any reserves or hesitation when he realised that God was calling him and Pauline to take over leadership at home. So Norman left Ibambi in 928 for that purpose.

Faithful Priscilla, "Mother Studd" to the large missionary family, enjoyed one last brief glimpse of her husband. On a casual impulse she arranged a visit to Egypt with a friend. Charles asked Norman to accompany her on the long journey from Khartoum, afraid that it might prove too great a strain for her. This Norman gladly did and the delight of the local Christians when "Mama Bwana" actually arrived made it all worthwhile. It helped them too to appreciate the sacrifice Charles had made in leaving his wife for years to bring the gospel to them. In the brief fortnight allowed to her, Priscilla spoke to the African converts many times through an interpreter. With the arrival of the hot season pending, she had to say farewell and return home with

Norman. It must have seemed particularly hard, knowing that they were unlikely ever to meet each other again on earth, but they bade each other goodbye in his bamboo hut and then she hurried off in the waiting motorcar without looking back. Soon after, Charles was notified of her sudden death while she was travelling in Spain with her friend, Mrs. Heber Radcliffe.

Charles wrote several tributes to her in letters after receiving the news. To Pauline, "My it was a shock. Mother is a great loss but she has won her reward. . . . We must now make good mother's place, we will not let the Lord's work fail or drag because God has so honoured her." To Stanley Smith, one of the original Cambridge Seven, "She was a wonder to many, but most of all to myself. She had such energy, vision and faith. . . . Well, she is a great loss, but I think she is doing a better work for God . . . than if she were down here, for she is with the Saviour, and I am quite sure He does not do much sleeping and so she won't either."

So for the final two years, Charles laboured on alone and yet he was surrounded by a loving family of forty missionaries, all very close to him and devoted to his interests. He for his part, made few personal demands upon them, his wants being few and his pleasures simple. By contrast he demanded a high standard of service for the Lord from them and exacted sacrificial giving in time and energy in their missionary duties.

The furnishings in his bamboo hut appeared sparse, offering little comfort. A native bed piled with threadbare khaki blankets and some thin, hard pillows occupied one corner. Nearby stood a table containing medicines and writing materials, opposite which was fixed a shelf full of used Bibles, Charles being in the habit of starting a fresh one each New Year to avoid being dependent on old notes and comments he had written in the margin.

An African houseboy curled up on the floor at night by an open log fire but rose at 3.00 am to make Bwana a cup of tea and then leave him alone with his Bible for a period of meditation. Often a long spell of practical work followed, quite often a new building project or repairs to timbers that had been ravaged by white ants. Again, Charles expected a professional standard of workmanship from the natives, impressing them that Christians spoiled their reputation by sloppy or lazy methods. People expected them to be consistent in their work and their witness, he told them. Often mealtimes would be disregarded to see a job through to fulfilment. At other times, he would spend hours at his table writing personal letters home or to other missionaries or bringing the accounts up to date. Only when all these activities were finished would he allow himself the supreme joy of setting out on an evangelistic trip. His luggage just took a short while to pack, consisting of spare clothes, a little food, blankets, a lantern, some medicines and his everpresent banjo. Usually a team of about ten men accompanied him. As long as he was able, Charles travelled on foot or by bicycle. It was merely in his latter years that he relied on native bearers to carry him along in a canvas chair with a protective cover of woven matting to keep off the worst of the sun and the rain. Often they walked through the night and stopped for a rest in the early hours, arriving in time to share breakfast with the missionaries at the outlying station.

News went out of his visits to surrounding settlements by means of drums and soon the forest trails were full of folk scuttling along, with their bundles, to the centre in order that they could hear Bwana. Time passed to enable as many as possible to reach there and then Charles led a session of lively singing with his banjo and finished with a Bible reading and gospel appeal. In between was fitted a short time of prayer, with as many as possible taking part in quick succession. Charles preferred to stand to give his address but towards the end of his life, he was compelled by weakness to support himself on his chair. And this could go on for days at a time. The weekend stretched out to several days and the sleeping huts became crammed with people who had come far to hear the word of life.

Well-meaning missionaries from time to time attempted to give Charles advice, only for his own good. "You really ought to travel back to England to have your teeth seen to, you've been having so much trouble with your remaining ones lately." To this Charles lightly replied, "If God intends me to be given some new ones, He can just as easily send some out here to me," and promptly relegated the topic to the back of his mind. But not so God. Within a few short months, a certain Mr. Buck, a dentist, in spite of being judged too old for work by the Committee at home, arrived in Ibambi with all the materials necessary for making Charles a new set. Unfortunately, the extractions were somewhat painful and at times Charles was forced to remove the dentures for a while to relieve the pressure on his sore gums. His old irrepressible sense of humour surfaced again and he derived great fun from mystifying the native Christians with his gleaming set of white teeth when he appeared at a Sunday morning service and then suddenly whipping them out and watching their incredulous faces!

Having more teeth meant that he could abandon his former mushy diet and eat a few more solids again. He benefited from this but other problems plagued him – fever, heart attacks, the old scourge of asthma and recurring indigestion. Charles did more translation work as he became less mobile. He even mastered a new language, Kingwana, which was used in the Ituri Province and assisted in the translation of the New Testament, the Psalms and extracts from the Proverbs. "I work an eighteen hour day," he wrote, "with no meals except what I gulp down as I write." As he dictated, Jack Harrison typed at his side and the result was a version so simple that any bush native who had learnt the basics of reading was able to understand it.

All this, of course, was at great cost to himself. Once in 1928 he was desperately ill for a whole week but he gradually recovered. From that time onwards, however, he became increasingly dependent on morphia, prescribed by missionary doctors who realised his particular circumstances and were confident he would use it sparingly and properly. No ordinary traditional course of treatment was available for him and it was only the morphia doses that kept him going. Needless to say, he came in for a good deal of criticism on this account, but there was really no alternative unless he had given everything up and travelled back to England for retirement and hospitalisation.

There were no regrets as he neared the end. In a letter home after summarising his life he stated firmly, "My only joys therefore are that when God has given me work to do, I have not refused it." Charles faced the situation squarely "My sands may run out any time." Then to his grandchildren he wrote, "I've been down to the River (of death) often lately; in fact I've lived in sight of the other shore these seven years. My loving advice to you is summed up in a few lines:

Only one life, 'twill soon be past;
Only what's done for Jesus will last.

In 1930, the King of the Belgians made him a Chevalier of the Royal Order of the Belgians in acknowledgement of his services to the Congo. He was also cheered and encouraged by native missionaries who were setting out to evangelise new, unreached areas.

In July, 1931, came the summons "Home." Jack Harrison filled in the details in a letter to Headquarters. On the 12th, Charles preached a five-hour sermon but from then on deteriorated and he passed away on the evening of the 16th. Characteristically, his last spoken word was "Hallelujah."

Local Christians worked all night to carve a coffin which was draped with the "Soldier-Saint" flag that Charles had designed. Hundreds filed past the coffin as it lay in the front room of his bamboo hut.

His daughter Edith supplied further pieces of information later. The day of his burial was stormy. Africans and whites alike were drenched by the torrential rain and even the giant forest trees were bowed and dripping in the storm.

After the funeral the crowds were reluctant to depart. Meetings followed on Saturday and by Sunday even larger crowds were meeting together. On the first anniversary of Charles' death a native conference was arranged at Ibambi. How many would turn up once Charles had gone? They need not have worried. Over seven thousand attended and the atmosphere was fantastic. Those present were led to renew their vows and rededicate themselves.

The work has gone on from strength to strength, a sure sign of the commitment of the founder. Fresh areas of work have opened up in different areas of the world. New volunteers keep coming forward to fill up the gaps. Further extensive accommodation has been provided as the old headquarters in London became inadequate. Great strides have been made too in the fields of literature evangelism. Nine hundred WEC missionaries serve Christ in over forty countries.

Charles' own words sum up his energetic and sacrificial life. "My heart is drumming with wonder at what God has done." This was his motivation to the end.

# THROUGH DAVID'S PSALMS

*Derek Prince*

Derek Prince, internationally known Bible teacher and scholar, draws on his understanding of the Hebrew language and culture, and a comprehensive knowledge of Scripture, to present 101 meditations from the Psalms.

Each of these practical and enriching meditations is based on a specific passage and concludes with a faith response. They can be used either for personal meditation or for family devotions. They are intended for all those who want their lives enriched or who seek comfort and encouragement from the Scriptures.

# LOVING GOD

*Charles Colson*

Loving God is the very purpose of the believer's life, the vocation for which he is made. However loving God is not easy and most people have given little real thought to what the greatest commandment really means.

Many books have been written on the individual subjects of repentence, Bible study, prayer, outreach, evangelism, holiness and other elements of the Christian life. In **Loving God**, Charles Colson draws all these elements together to look at the entire process of growing up as a Christian.

Combining vivid illustrations with straightforward exposition he shows how to live out the Christian faith in our daily lives. **Loving God** provides a real challenge to deeper commitment and points the way towards greater maturity.

# THE TORN VEIL

*Sister Gulshan and Thelma Sangster*

Gulshan Fatima was brought up in a Muslim Sayed family according to the orthodox Islamic code of the Shias.

Suffering from a crippling paralysis she travelled to England in search of medical help. Although unsuccessful in medical terms, this trip marked the beginning of a spiritual awakening that led ultimately to her conversion to Christianity.

Gulshan and her father also travelled to Mecca in the hope that God would heal her, but that trip too was of no avail. However, Gulshan was not detered. She relentlessly pursued God and He faithfully answered her prayers. Her conversion, when it came, was dramatic and brought with a miraculous healing.

**The Torn Veil** is Sister Gulshan's thrilling testimony to the power of God which can break through every barrier.


# NOW I CALL HIM BROTHER

*Alec Smith*

Alec Smith, son of Ian Smith the rebel Prime Minister of Rhodesia whose Unilateral Declaration of Independence plunged his country into twelve years of bloody racial war, has written his own story of those years.

The story of his life takes him from early years of rebellion against his role as 'Ian Smith's son' through his youth as a drop-out, hippy and drug peddler into the Rhodesian forces.

A dramatic Christian conversion experience at the height of the civil war transformed his life and led to the passionate conviction to see reconciliation and peace in a deeply divided country.

What follows is a thrilling account of how God can take a dedicated life and help to change the course of history.

If you wish to receive *regular information* about *new books*, please send your name and address to:

London Bible Warehouse
PO Box 123
Basingstoke
Hants RG23 7NL

Name........................................................................................................

Address ...............................................................................................

........................................................................................................

........................................................................................................

........................................................................................................

I am especially interested in:
☐ Biographies
☐ Fiction
☐ Christian living
☐ Issue related books
☐ Academic books
☐ Bible study aids
☐ Children's books
☐ Music
☐ Other subjects

P.S. If you have ideas for new Christian Books or other products, please write to us too!